Advance Accolades

"I'm not sure how I sold ANYTHING before I started using Michael's system! He has amazing insight and a proven approach that can turn any sales manager into a true leader that gets results.

This book is a blueprint for sales management success. Read it, follow it, and become a disciple of this system."
—**Brian Waller**, President and CEO
of **Insurance Finance Company**

"Michael has demystified sales management and given his readers a simple approach that just works. There is no fluff, filler, or BS in this book—it's not your normal list of 50 sales tips and traps.

The tools and processes are comprehensive and strategic, AND quick to implement for high-impact results. Michael Andersen does for sales managers what Patrick Lencioni did for teams!"
—**Jim Horan**, author of *The One Page Business Plan*

"What a great behind-the-scenes look at running a sales team! The characters and situations in the story are fully relatable to real-life situations. And the solutions have proven extremely effective in my own experience, as I am sure they will for other readers.

The best practices detailed in this book will improve your team's effectiveness, accountability, and overall financial results and create a collaborative culture that makes everyone's work more enjoyable."
—**Tom MacManus**, former CEO North America Operations,
GMAC Commercial Mortgage

"This book is fun to read and packs powerful lessons that every sales manager and CEO needs to understand. Too many midsized company CEOs blame the salespeople when they could get far better results by looking more closely at how the team is set up for success.

Andersen does a great job of laying out one action plan after another for helping a sales team consistently deliver a mighty performance. This is a mandatory read for sales managers and CEOs who wants more predictable sales."

—**Robert Sher**, author of *Mighty Midsized Companies* and Columnist at **Forbes.com**

"Absolutely brilliant! The system of sales management proposed is very common sense, yet so uncommon in companies today.

You cannot read the story and the takeaway sections without thinking 'Well, of course!'... followed immediately by 'I can't believe I didn't think of this before!' This book provides a fabulous roadmap for development and motivation so you can lead a sales team to great success."

—**Michael Beach**, former Executive Director of Global Channel Operations, **Dell**

For a sales manager, this book overflows with invaluable wisdom. I know because I used Michael's strategies to develop the #1 regional sales team for my former employer. And now as president of a young company, I've used them to go from zero to exceeding our ambitious sales goals.

I've read 100+ sales books, and a lot of them re-hash the same ideas. This book takes a fresh and detailed look at the challenges of getting teams to rethink sales production. It's a tremendous asset that I refer back to all the time. I know our success depends on predictable sales results, and this book delivers on that promise.

—**David Handsaker**, President and CEO of **Growers Axis**, a subsidiary of Wilbur-Ellis

I have decades of successful experience as a sales manager, but reading *A Culture of Predictable Sales* opened my eyes to a whole new realm of opportunity. I realized I'd been relying on old strategies, gut instincts, and my own personal experiences.

Applying the practical strategies and tools presented throughout this book, I've seen incredible benefits in a very short time. Michael Andersen does a masterful job teaching the "art" and "science" of sales management. This truly is a must-read—it's outstanding and it works!

—**Jon Denney**, Sales Vice President of
NightRider Janitorial Services, Inc.

Michael Andersen is one of the smartest sales minds today. I know from firsthand experience just how well his system works in the real world. And now he's turned his vast knowledge into a priceless resource for business owners, sales leaders, and sales managers.

The true-to-life story immediately draws you in, and the takeaway chapters help you dissect and understand the concepts and strategies. This is an outstanding book that belongs in every sales manager's briefcase! "

—**Larry Lewis**, top sales consultant and
author of *Client Builder Selling*

A Culture of Predictable Sales

One Sales Manager's Journey

Michael Andersen

Essentia Business Publishing
500 West Hickman Road #772
Waukee, IA 50263
www.essentiaba.com

ISBN: 978-1-7339348-0-0

Printed in the United States of America.

Acknowledgements

Writing a book is much harder than I thought and more rewarding than I could have ever imagined. I have been often reminded that "I can do all things through Christ who strengthens me." God has purpose in everything he directs us to do in our lives if we seek Him and accept His Lordship. This experience has truly been a blessing for me, and I trust that it can be used by Him as a blessing in others' lives as well.

I'd like to start by thanking all of you who directly helped me in compiling my thoughts, editing my writing, illustrating my ideas, and polishing the form and style of this book. I could not have accomplished writing this book without your support. Benjamin Conboy, I have been so enriched through our work together on this book. In many ways, this is your first book too.

To my editors Craig Lancaster, Megan Dougherty, and Jim Thomsen, I wish to thank each of you for the patience you extended to me as we worked simultaneously through my lack of experience and insistence that we get it right no matter what it takes. Special thanks to Alexandra Vezure, Sean Conboy, and Cheri Lasota for showing me that good form is an imperative partner to good substance. You transformed the book's aesthetics.

To all the individuals I have had the opportunity to lead, to coach, to work with, or be mentored by, I want to say thank you for being the inspiration and foundation for both the story portion of this book and the learning opportunities that informed the takeaway portions. I know that the content of this book has come through my many failures and instructional opportunities with you all. Although, over the years, I have been blessed with many such relationships, I would like to point out just a few that have stood out most: Doug Nicolet, Tim Ganske, Don Doudna, David Creighton, Sr., George Suskalo, Tim Gifford, Kevin Fields, Scott Green, Corbin Winter, Bruce Brinick, Jim Lobaito, Christian Comito, Andrea Westmeyer, Larry Lewis, Jim Campbell, Jon Denney, Doug Flugum, Dave Handsaker, Jerry Dunn, and Jim Wiginton. Thanks to you all for such rich learning experiences.

Besides these individuals, I must also thank especially my father, Dan Andersen. Beyond delivering the most privileged and blessed upbringing a son could desire, you have in so many tremendous ways inspired and supported me through all of my life. In my childhood days you always devoted time to my incessant questions about your management experiences with the teams you led. As a young adult, you modeled what a true mentor and leader does through your Godly servant leadership style of parenting. And, now, your continued sacrifice and dedication to me in so many ways is phenomenal. Thanks from the bottom of my heart for being a catalyst (and first editor) for this book.

Also, many thanks to my two beautiful, remarkable, and devoted daughters, Brittany and Emily. You are the inspiration for my life, and I could not have mustered the energy for this project without your love and support.

Finally, to my thoughtful, loving, and supportive wife, Joleen: my deepest gratitude. Your assistance, encouragement, and unwavering trust in me through it all have been invaluable. I know that not only this book, but all of the career experience that backs it up, would not have been possible without you.

Visit *A Culture Of Predictable Sales* Resource Companion Website Today!

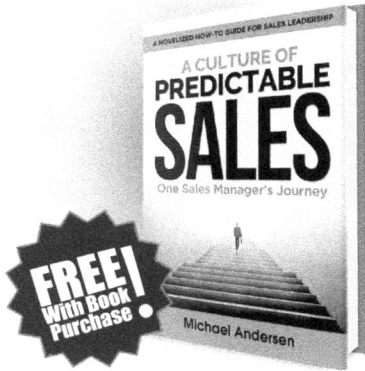

This website is full of valuable resources and downloadable content that you can use immediately. These resources are designed to reinforce the lessons learned by Rolland in a way that you can apply them in your current sales management role today.

Start Using these Tools Now, While You Read the Book.

✔ Sales Focus Blueprint™ Template
✔ One-on-One Debrief Form
✔ OnBoarding Form
✔ Pre-Call Plan Form
✔ Team Balloon Model™
✔ Coaching Spectrum™
✔ Account Management Matrix™
✔ Mentorship Ladder™
✔ And More

To Find These Resources and Many More Go To:

Table of Contents

INTRODUCTION
A Company at a Crossroads

ROLLAND MANDAT WATCHED DOM DIAZ, WHO WAS RUNNING FINGERS through his hair and collecting his thoughts. Rolland knew his boss well, respected him, and could sense the frustration sparking off him. When at last Dom spoke again, his eyes locked on Rolland's.

"You've got to generate greater results, now." Rolland nodded. He knew the score, but he didn't dare interrupt the rest of what he knew was coming.

"Rolland," Dom went on, "I've put my reputation and money on the line this past year. I promoted you to lead the team, and I borrowed more money six months ago to finance our new CRM system and kick-start our expansion." His grim visage softened now, along with his voice. "It's not like Arachnid is taking on water. I still believe you're the man for this job and that you can create the growth we're looking for."

Rolland's thoughts traveled back a year and a half, to when Dom had promoted him. Arachnid had been on the cusp of something big, something far beyond the two-person startup it had once been. Arachnid Technology, with headquarters in Kansas City, was now one of the metro area's leading technology-solutions providers and had recently expanded to Springfield to further the brand. Rolland had appreciated the confidence shown in him by his boss—just as he'd appreciated being hired in the first place ten years earlier when he was jobless and needed a break.

He owed much to Dom and didn't want to let him down now.

"I agree, Dom," he said. "Sales have been less than desired. But if there's one thing I know how to do, it's to sell Arachnid Technology. We'll get those numbers up even if I have to go out and do so myself. Not to mention, Brad's got a deal brewing, and last I heard Janet was going out to do a presentation this afternoon with a great new opportunity."

As Rolland attempted to impart confidence to Dom, he couldn't help but reflect on the last couple of months leading to this point. He had always produced reliable sales for Arachnid, so why was he facing this predicament? Dom was asking for forward-looking answers, and Rolland fought against himself as he dwelled on the past in his effort to understand. The clock on the wall behind Dom was ticking so slowly that time seemed to be standing still for Rolland as his mind drifted away and recounted the recent events.

Many challenges loomed. On one hand, Rolland had been commissioned by Dom to set up and utilize a new CRM system. On the other, he had a mixed bag of salespeople to manage as well as an open position he'd been trying to fill for the past nine months. Brad Graham, the salesman he'd just talked up to Dom, was a particular struggle because he seemed much more willing to assist with the CRM implementation than fulfill his sales duties.

Rolland looked to Dom again. "We're going to get it done," he said.

"I know," Dom replied.

O N THE WALK BACK TO HIS OFFICE, ROLLAND AGAIN THOUGHT ABOUT Brad and their last review meeting.

"What's the latest on your opportunity with Serbo Manufacturing?" Rolland had asked.

Brad, as ever, struck an optimistic tone. "We are making significant progress. The prospect has invited me over a few times and I've gotten to explain the ins and outs of network security to him and how he'd benefit from such a system. I'm telling you, Rolland, this guy was clueless before I came along. I already scheduled our next call to discuss what he should expect in terms of timeline and difficulty when it comes to converting his current network over."

Rolland shook his head at the memory. Arachnid was Brad's third sales job in four years since his graduation from Northwest Missouri State, and it was safe to say he hadn't set the world ablaze in any of them. At Arachnid, he'd inherited a couple of customers but hadn't grown their business. With the arrival of the CRM system, Brad's tendencies to learn and teach had been engaged, but his primary function—selling—had continued to be less than optimum.

Rolland realized now that he'd let Brad continue on that path in the meeting.

"All right," Rolland had said. "It sounds like you're still in the game and closing in on a potential deal. Assuming your upcoming call is a success, let's shoot to have a proposal wrapped up and submitted by the end of the month."

Rolland slipped now into his chair and began making notes about the meeting with Dom and about the other challenges Arachnid faced. The hurdles, he figured, were considerable. So, too, were the potential rewards. He had to get this going in the right direction again.

THE STORY OF ARACHNID WAS LORE TO EVERYONE WHO WORKED THERE. Dom Diaz and his brother Carlos founded the firm out of Dom's basement. Dom had several years of experience selling computer repair and small-office networks.

The big break, the one that launched the company, had been one Dom never saw coming. A guy had called, saying he needed some assistance with his Sprint cellular integrating into the work network for document sharing. Dom figured him for a small-business owner who wanted to use his smartphone in a better way. When Dom arrived for the job, he found himself at Sprint headquarters, being asked to be a vendor on a team that was integrating its newest phone device for business customers.

It turned out that Dom and Carlos' gregarious uncle, Enrique, who worked at IBM, had given Sprint the referral. From there, Dom continued to grow his network and expertise through that project and many more before risking it all and starting his own company, Arachnid Technology. Carlos, as the behind-the-scenes brain of the operation, wasn't much of a salesman but was an extremely valuable VP of Service, given his tech knowledge. Arachnid became something big, and fast. And now it was a stumbling a bit as it tried to become something even bigger.

Rolland, still working through his thoughts, considered his team. Enrique Dumas, Dom and Carlos' uncle, was Arachnid's best salesperson, with more experience than anybody else in the building. His years with IBM had exposed him to some of the best sales training of the time from the likes of Brian Tracy, Zig Ziglar, and others. After Enrique's original referral of his nephews to Sprint, they'd asked him to come aboard at Arachnid, and he'd persuaded Sprint to accompany him and move its business over. He was, as everyone knew, essential to the team. He was also closing in on retirement and, perhaps, was resistant to new ideas.

Rolland remembered how he had referenced this earlier with Dom: "While we might be positioning ourselves for when Enrique retires, I also fully intend to leverage his skills while he's still part of the team. We discussed going on a couple of calls together over the coming weeks—we make one heck of a dynamic duo!" It had been a moment of optimism, where he'd bought into Dom's confidence and believed his team was in a firm position to bring in new business.

Rolland, as he closed up his office and prepared to head home, resolved to carry that optimism through to the next day.

WHILE ROLLAND AND HIS WIFE WAITED FOR THEIR MEAL AT ONE OF THEIR favorite places, Sal's BBQ, he shared his day. He'd been buoyant since leaving work, eager to validate Dom's confidence in him.

"Today was a bad day, but it was also a good day." When his wife's face scrunched up at the competing thoughts, Rolland scrambled to shore up his meaning.

"Dom really got me thinking," he said. "He's not pleased, and I can't blame him. We've had to adjust my sales plan each of the last three quarters. But still, I'm feeling strong about a few irons we have in the fire."

Audrey Mandat sipped from her iced tea. "You've always been good at this, Rolland."

"Yeah," Rolland said, his excitement rising. "But it's not just me. There's Janet. She's so driven. In fact, right before my meeting with Dom, she came up and filled me in on her afternoon presentation. I didn't have much time, but I could feel her excitement. The thing is, I know I need to spend more time with her, helping her fine-tune certain skills. Like today, I had to remind her not to hand out the presentation packets until she was finished with her pitch. But that drive, that's something I can't teach. She has it."

Janet Applegate was a true rookie in the sales business, but she had come from a successful background. As a college cheerleader, she walked with pep in her step and never shied from competition.

Since the day she was hired, Rolland believed she was a natural-born seller. She may have lacked technical knowledge, but Janet could build rapport like the best of them. Rolland was sure the technical details could be taught over time.

The plate of ribs arrived, and the Mandats dug in.

Dinner was what Rolland hoped it would be, a chance to reconnect with the fullness of his life in a place full of happy memories. Work was a struggle now, but a worthwhile one. And he had support there, and at home.

His wife had been there through everything—the hard early years, when he was looking for traction; the unemployment; the revival of his career and prospects with Arachnid. Without his having to say anything, Rolland knew she understood the situation he was in now, and that buoyed him further.

After the meal was finished, the server came around, and Rolland said, "We'd like some apple cobbler. And if possible, would you put an extra scoop of ice cream on there for my lovely lady?"

They drove home, full and happy and talking in anticipation of big moments to come for their family. As Rolland parked the car at home, he said to his wife, "It's a good life, isn't it?"

"The best," she replied.

R OLLAND ARRIVED AT WORK THE NEXT DAY STILL ON A HIGH. HE GREETED his receptionist, Sarah, with bravado as he entered the building.

"That must have been some song on the radio," Sarah said, smiling at him.

"The song is in my heart, Sarah," he said. "In my heart."

As he breezed by, she said, "Don't forget you've got…"

That brought him tumbling back into work and out of his reverie. "Right," he said. "But, listen, you'll have to reschedule those for me. Today, I'm working with Enrique. Could you also inform the team we'll have a sales meeting at the end of the day, along with Carlos?"

"I'm on it," Sarah said.

Rolland moved along, his purpose clear. He'd worn his crisply starched white shirt and red tie that day. His power outfit. Rolland believed that you couldn't beat a classic look. Dressing to impress meant one thing—that he was going out in the field to sit in front of prospects personally.

When Enrique joined him, Rolland set about his first task. He felt like he was in an old Western movie, where he was the sheriff and Enrique was his trusted deputy, and they were strutting slowly toward the end of town to greet a band of desperadoes. The rest of the Arachnid sales team was like the townspeople, watching in wonder as they walked by.

And sure enough, it was like old times out in the field. Rolland knew he and Enrique brought distinct values to each sales call. Enrique was the wise, old-school veteran with the family ties to the business. Rolland was the wheeler and dealer.

Together, they closed their first deal of the day by lunch. It was like old times for Rolland. When the pressure was on, he became personally invested in making sales. This deal was a shimmer of hope. Rolland had that spark inside him again. It was his killer instinct that gave Dom the confidence to promote him in the first place.

AS THE DAY DREW TO A CLOSE, ROLLAND GATHERED THE SALES TEAM AND Carlos. His goal was to bring enough of his own gusto to the meeting and pass it on to the team. He borrowed Dom's words to kick things off: "Now is our time! Just this morning Enrique and I went out and closed a large deal. All we have to do is keep grinding. Dom is looking for more growth, and I don't think his expectations are misplaced. You all have the tools for the job, so let's make it happen."

He turned to Janet, full of expectations. "You just had a presentation at Peace of Mind Insurance yesterday, right? Why don't you share how that went with the group."

When the dark cloud crossed Janet's face, Rolland knew he'd put her uncomfortably on the spot. Still, she gathered herself, stood, and made her report.

"Well … I had put together a great presentation," she said, looking to Rolland and smiling in a way that he sensed was forced. "I was ready to show them the benefits of our network solutions and how they would solve all their problems. My contact, Jim, and I had a handful of positive correspondences leading up to yesterday, so I was looking forward to a simple walk-through presentation with him."

Rolland gently prompted her to keep going. "OK, sounds good."

"But when I arrived," Janet said, "Jim told me that the president was going to join us and was very interested in my presentation. I was brought into the boardroom and asked if I needed to connect to the monitor. I said *no* because I had only anticipated discussing my quote and had brought along only a single copy of the presentation. As I tried to walk through the presentation, I was really worried that I'd embarrassed Jim because the president wanted to know all of these technical details that I didn't have answers prepared for.

"The president's comment as I left was, 'When you have a chance to get all of the information together, would you let us know? We're interested in seeing all of it.' I was hoping to talk to you, Rolland, and see how to redirect the situation."

"Oh." Rolland was rattled, no two ways about it, but he stepped up the energy again because he didn't want to lose positivity in the room. "Not to worry, Janet, we all have our days. The deal doesn't sound like it's completely lost just yet. If their president wants to get involved, maybe it would be best for us to have a manager in the room, too. How about we schedule another presentation, and this time I'll come with you?" Janet nodded, again smiling, and sat down. Rolland made the pivot. "What else is going on that we should discuss?"

Brad dove in. "Well, I've made some really great progress on the CRM system. We did some testing yesterday and I think we're just about ready to turn on the marketing module. By the way, I did get a call the other day from Cerner. They seemed to be concerned about a delivery. Enrique was out so I did the best I could to support them. It took quite a bit of time out of my day—"

Enrique interrupted.

"Stop right there, OK, Brad," he said. "I'd be happy to take care of my own customer's concerns. But, you know what the real problem is, Rolland? I was out trying to deliver a quote and got waylaid into a lengthy conversation about how high the quote was. Lately it seems like our quotes aren't connecting because they just aren't competitive."

"That's true," Janet agreed.

"Can't argue there," Brad tossed in.

Enrique went on. "I'm not sure what's going on down in Tech Services, but the quotes they're giving us to take to our prospects are way overboard. We should only be quoting them according to what they are actually asking for. We should be delivering only a solution based on what the client needs—not whatever solution

Tech Services views as *perfect* based on their engineering. We need them to start listening to us and the customer more if we're going to be successful."

Rolland looked toward Carlos, sensing what was coming. These observations landed directly in his lap.

"You people just don't know what you're doing out there," Carlos said, and Rolland cringed. "If you understood what it takes to provide a quality technical solution better, you would be able to pitch the customers more appropriately. Customers expect scalable, secure, and reliable solutions. If we delivered what you sometimes want us to quote, we'd be out on our ear!"

As the voices rose, Rolland cut in and ended the meeting. "Let's leave it at that for now." Still, his sales team protested Carlos's knock against them, and Rolland said, "Look, Carlos and I will meet separately and talk about strategies for better solution alignment and, perhaps, better technical training if it's necessary. All right?"

Everybody filed out. Rolland hung back to clear his head. It wasn't the meeting he had hoped for, and he felt his earlier energy continue to drain out. He also tried to hold on to the positives: He'd pushed a message across to his team, there were new directives to attack, and he was looking forward to collaborations with Carlos and with Janet.

THE FOLLOWING WEDNESDAY, ROLLAND AND JANET SET OUT TO SAVE what they could of her deal. Rolland felt good about the opportunity here: With his tenure and experience, not to mention his managerial status, the president would better respect him, and he could keep an open discussion going. At the same time, Janet would have a chance to show what she could do. He looked forward to seeing her in action.

As Rolland and Janet arrived at Peace of Mind Insurance, they received a perfunctory and terse greeting in the lobby. As they took their seats, he asked Janet, "Are they always this cold?"

"No," Janet admitted. Rolland thought he sensed she had more to say, but when she went no further, he let it go.

Soon, they were ushered into the boardroom, shown their seats, and given directions on how to connect their presentation to the monitor. While they were waiting, Rolland said, "Now, just so we're clear, I want to be the one to initiate any discussions about pricing or how we've structured our solution. I think that would be better coming from the sales manager. Wouldn't you agree?"

Janet nodded. "When I get to that part of the presentation, I'll make sure to include you." As the last word cleared her lips, Jim and the company president walked in. Rolland realized he and Janet were not on the same page, but it was too late for a course correction.

After a brief meet-and-greet, Janet called the meeting to order. She began with an apology about the previous presentation and said she now had the technical information the company sought. She then opened a PowerPoint presentation on her laptop.

Rolland sat, quiet and dismayed. He thought he'd asked her to keep the meeting an open forum for questions and answers. That would give them time to gauge when Rolland and the company president should talk executive-to-executive.

Instead, here was Janet with a lengthy, technical analysis of all the benefits that the customer could gain by moving forward with the project. While this was all true, Rolland thought it was better suited for a presentation to the tech team than to the president. It seemed Janet had misinterpreted the president's interest in hearing about business solutions as wanting more information on highly technical integration features.

Rolland was in a bind. He was certain Janet wasn't giving the client what it wanted, yet he couldn't just dive across the table and stop her.

As Janet got to her fourth slide, the president broke in with a question. "I understand your solution is well-engineered technically," he said. "At the same time, we can only afford so much. What will this cost us anyway?"

Rolland interpreted this succinctly: *When will we get to the point?* Before Rolland could assert some control and redirect things, Janet started answering. Ignoring their strategy and Rolland's reminder before the call, Janet divulged what a top-to-bottom package would cost, the biggest deal she could put on the table.

The president closed his notebook. "I'm sure you guys have a great solution for a company ten times our size," he said. "But based on the costs you just gave me, I don't believe we need to discuss this plan further."

The drive back to the office was mostly brutal silence. For a moment,

Janet was apologetic, and while Rolland appreciated that, he remained irritated.

"How could you get in my way like that?" he asked. "We came off as fools presenting stuff they didn't want to hear and throwing prices at them that were completely out of their ballpark. You came into this job with so much potential, Janet. What happened?"

"I'm sorry," Janet said again.

The two remained quiet, and the question—*what happened?*—hung there between them. The only noises the rest of the way to the office were Rolland's teeth grinding, the heavy raindrops on the windshield, and the squeaky wiper blades trying to keep pace with the downpour. As they pulled back into the lot at Arachnid, Rolland handed Janet the umbrella from the back seat and said, "We'll get 'em next time."

Rolland got back into his office and hung his wet coat over the back of his chair. He let out a heavy sigh as he tried to reconstruct how everything went wrong. Several minutes passed, and Rolland was still gazing blankly out his window. Then, out the corner of his eye he noticed the blinking light on his telephone, signifying a voicemail.

"Hello, Mr. Mandat. This is Elise over at Cerner. I know Enrique's been busy lately, but my boss was asking me to get some details on the latest network update. Last time I was able to get Brad on the line to help, but he wasn't available, so I thought maybe it'd be quicker to ask you directly. Feel free to call anytime this afternoon. Thanks for your assistance."

Rolland saved the message. Cerner was one of Arachnid's biggest clients. Enrique had signed the company years ago and had a great relationship with upper management. Nobody from Cerner had a sour thing to say about him, and they were always willing to give glowing recommendations to other prospects. Rolland thought it strange that Elise had reached out to him. He had never micromanaged the account and had few conversations with Cerner outside of being introduced by Enrique following his promotion to sales manager.

Rolland caught Enrique at his desk.

"Hey, Enrique, I just got a call from Cerner inquiring about our latest update. What's the word on their account?"

The star salesman picked up the thread quickly. "Oh, right," he confirmed. "I've been meaning to get in touch with them. I had a conversation with them not long ago, but apparently they need more information. I'm sure everything is fine. I'll call them right up. Thanks for letting me know!"

"No problem," Rolland said. Enrique went back to his work. Rolland paused, considering. "I know how you feel about the CRM system," Rolland began.

"Yeah?" Enrique said, looking up. He had a tentative look on his face.

"It's just that one of the things where it really helps is keeping track of when you reach out to clients. I just thought I'd mention it."

"Come on, Rolland," Enrique said, brushing him back. "I don't need Big Brother watching my accounts. I've gotten this far without it, so what's the point? CRM probably works great for people like Brad and Janet who need a lot of help. But if Arachnid is expanding so fast that people can't keep track of their own business, then it probably shouldn't scale as quickly. I don't see how that's my issue."

Rolland looked for a soft exit. "I get it. Just following up."

"I'll call them," Enrique said. "Don't worry about it."

Rolland said his thanks and hung up. Amid everything, he figured he had to trust his top performer. Too many other fires demanded his immediate attention.

Brad Graham, for example. Several weeks had passed and Rolland wanted to inspect the status of Brad's latest prospect, so he brought Brad in for a one-on-one session. Rolland got to it quickly. "Brad, you told me that you'd be closing Serbo Manufacturing by now. Has that happened?"

"Not exactly," Brad said. "I've been pretty tied down recently—you know, the CRM implementation—so I haven't followed up. I'm going to now. However, we did have another great meeting with them. We covered conversion expectations as you and I discussed and it went wonderfully. I told him all about our case studies and the great success we've had, and I explained what the next steps should be to get him to the point where he's ready to implement our system. He seemed very engaged and grateful for my time."

"How long was this meeting?" Rolland asked.

"Probably about an hour."

Rolland bottom-lined it. "It sounds to me like you're giving away a lot of free consulting, not closing the deal. Didn't we talk about this? I remember telling you it was time to submit a proposal and get the deal signed. Weren't you listening during our team meeting? We need action."

"Oh, no, I've got him on the ropes!" Brad insisted. "The last time I was in he even told me that his daughter thought I was charming. Of course, I pointed out the ring on my finger—"

"I've heard this fluff before, Brad. What will it take to get you to start signing new customers?"

As Rolland dwelled on that question, awaiting an answer he wasn't sure he'd get, he couldn't help but consider the easy solution: let Brad go. That math collided with other parts of the equation, though. He had an open position to fill and a top performer who was close to retirement. Now wasn't the time to go down another salesperson.

In the absence of an answer from Brad, Rolland filled the silence. "I'm handcuffed here, Brad. I need you to get on board with the plan. I don't know what else to say."

Brad left the office, and Rolland dropped his head in defeat. The sales forecast was open on his computer, the projections more daunting by the minute. There was no way Dom would be comfortable with the numbers. The forecast was reliant on too many uncertainties. Janet's deal was a bust despite Rolland's best efforts. Even though Brad was in denial, Rolland knew his deal was also as good as dead. And then there was Enrique. Sure, he'd always been reliable, but it was a tall task to accurately project his sales when there was nothing entered into the CRM system.

Rolland opened a blank Word document. He watched his cursor flash on and off the screen. He wondered if he shouldn't draft his resignation. His fingers lingered above the keyboard, but nothing came.

Rolland closed the document and left his office.

"I'M AT A LOSS, DOM," ROLLAND BEGAN. HE'D DECIDED TO BE DIRECT, unflinching. His boss, the guy who'd given him a career when Rolland was at his lowest ebb, deserved it.

"The last time we spoke I felt more confident about my ability to turn the team around," Rolland continued. "I even went out and did some selling on my own like I used to. The CRM system is great. But at the same time it's a distraction to Brad, who needs to be out selling, and it's detestable to Enrique, who would actually benefit from it. And Janet ... Janet, Janet, Janet."

Dom looked to him, as if to say, *Tell me more.*

"She was supposed to be our up-and-comer, but she's scuttling deals with rookie mistakes," Rolland said. "I know this isn't what you were looking for, Dom. I don't want to keep letting you down. It might be best for Arachnid if you hire a sales manager who can turn this thing around and let me go contribute more in sales where I'm doing well. Maybe I would best serve this company by doing that."

Dom set his hands on the desk in front of him, entwining his fingers. He offered a soft smile.

"I have the utmost trust in you, Rolland. I've been watching from a distance. Perhaps I promoted you too quickly without enough support."

"Yeah, maybe," Rolland said. "I know my resume says I have previous experience as a sales manager, but that title at 3Com was more of a lead-from-the-front position. I mean, they really mapped the whole road out for me."

"A totally different role compared to managing a small team at a growing entrepreneurial business." Dom smiled again. "But remember, Rolland, it's not like you've completely failed. I don't see the future as gloomily as you currently do. Janet had a significant misstep, but she still shows great promise. Enrique is set in his ways and may need reminding of certain tasks, but he's still closing new deals. Didn't you both recently have a major success together? As for Brad, you're right. He probably does need to go his own way, but that's partially why we need to hire a new salesperson first.

"I have been thinking. It may be a good idea to bring an outside consultant to work with and mentor you. Someone who has an objective view and can help you further develop your strengths and get them focused in the right areas for success. They will guide you and your team down the path of least resistance so you can make smoother progress. Would you be open to that?"

Rolland brightened. He'd come to this meeting expecting to resign or be self-demoted. Dom was suggesting something entirely different.

"I've always been a lifelong learner and I enjoy learning about better ways to do things," Rolland said. "If you think this will be valuable, I'd sure be willing to try it."

Dom stood and came to Rolland's side of the desk. "I'm glad that's how you feel. I've actually been in contact with a consultant already, because I wanted to understand for myself what he has to offer to you. As you said, bringing on a consultant doesn't mean that I've lost faith in you. In fact, it means I have a lot of faith in you because I'm willing to make the investment."

"I appreciate that," Rolland said. "I won't let you down."

Dom went on. "I know you won't. I believe there is an easier way to move the team forward than having you reinvent the wheel the hard way. You're a smart guy, Rolland, which is why you're in the position you hold. You'd have figured it out eventually. I think this will help get to that resolution faster."

* * *

AUTHOR'S NOTE: *ROLLAND MANDAT IS A FICTIONAL CHARACTER BASED ON various sales managers I've worked with over many years of coaching. As the story goes on, the consultant—Monroe—will provide coaching to Rolland that will address a number of issues he has dealt with. Each chapter will highlight characters and issues central to Rolland's challenges as he learns to rethink his approach to management and guide his team to success.*

You may not be facing all of these same challenges, but this story has aspects all of us can relate to. Rolland is confronted with real struggles that I have seen managers deal with or that I have come up against in my own businesses. Often, we get so focused on our own involvement in sales that we don't spend enough time passing along what we've learned. Other times, our plans and agendas for meetings aren't as strong as they could be. We always have challenges, but we don't always have the answers.

When I sat down to write, my thought was to share the common issues and concerns that I have seen and experienced through my career. I wanted to then provide a true how-to guide for navigating these challenges. So my first book, **Intentional Sales Management (ISM),** *provided a complete methodology for achieving predictable sales results. This book takes the next step and shows the practical application of those concepts, providing a demonstration of a fully intentional approach to management.*

Other resources I've accessed have provided various tips and a potpourri of ideas on how to be better managers. All of these are good and helpful, but I felt that having a complete system, integrated from top to bottom and covering all the necessary areas of sales management, would be valuable to readers. The key to having predictable sales is to start with an intentional system.

As you read on, consider each concept discussed, as it applies to the totality of the process. In seminars I've attended and books I've read, I've

Introduction

found that if I can pull out even one nugget of wisdom that will benefit my business, the effort has been worthwhile. I trust you will discover similar success by reading and implementing the Intentional Sales process that is demonstrated here, and that your experience with this book will enhance your own journey. I would wish you good luck, but luck is a fleeting thing. Instead, Godspeed as you chart your course ahead with intentional sales management!

CHAPTER ONE

The Sales Manager's New Ally

A<small>T THE START OF A NEW DAY, A NEW WEEK,</small> R<small>OLLAND PULLED INTO THE</small> parking lot at Arachnid Technology and took note of a vehicle he hadn't seen there before. It was a sleek black sedan—late-model and upper-end, but not overly flashy.

"Must be Monroe," Rolland said to himself as he swung into his own space. "Here nice and early. I like it."

Over the weekend, Rolland had ruminated on the changes coming to Arachnid. He'd maintained the attitude he had imparted to Dom—he really was eager to see what an outside consultant could bring to the organization, and to Rolland's performance specifically. But he was nervous, too, in the way anyone is when unknown change is in the air. At 3Com, Rolland had worked with an internal management coach, someone who administered a whole program for managers. The coach was a resource for working through different processes and management techniques.

But this would be something new and different. At the door, Rolland took a deep breath, then headed in.

Sarah, as ever, greeted him. "Good morning," she said. "Dom is waiting for you in the conference room." She lowered her voice to a concerned whisper. "He's in there with the new consultant."

"Thank you, Sarah."

No wasting time, Rolland thought. *Good. The way it should be.*

Rolland made a brief stop at his office to set down his things and do one last bit of steeling himself for the coming meeting. He gave himself a pep talk; "This is the moment of truth. Dom deserves to reach the next level with Arachnid. So do I. Here we go."

"GENTLEMEN," ROLLAND SAID UPON ENTERING THE CONFERENCE ROOM. Dom and Monroe stood at the far end of the table, talking as if they were old chums. Rolland sized up Monroe. He was professionally dressed, but not in a way that was over the top—the right touch for a smaller company like Arachnid. He strode toward Rolland with hand extended, smiling and then speaking in a low, resonant voice, one that blended warmth and authority. "Monroe," the consultant said cheerfully, introducing himself. "You must be Rolland."

"A pleasure to meet you," Rolland said, gripping Monroe's offered hand.

Dom invited them to sit.

"I'm excited about this," Dom said. "Monroe has over twenty-five years of experience in sales and works with companies in situations like ours all of the time. He's worked at Fortune 100 companies, and comes highly recommended. In fact, Rolland, I was just getting around to telling him how long you've been with Arachnid and how we met."

"Ten years," Rolland said, looking to Monroe and then back to Dom. "It's been quite a ride."

"I'll bet," Monroe said.

Dom now focused his gaze on Monroe. "This man is a dedicated lieutenant," he said, sweeping his hand to indicate Rolland. "He will do whatever it takes to succeed. He'll be a sponge, so give him plenty to soak up."

"I'm looking forward to it," Monroe said, and Rolland nodded in assent.

"As both of you well know, we absolutely must be successful," Dom said. "There's a lot on the line. I'm leaving it to you, together, to find the way forward."

With that, Dom stood up and departed, leaving Rolland and Monroe to work through the formalities and get down to the details. Rolland felt the fluttering in his stomach subside a bit. Dom was an able boss, one who spoke directly and succinctly and then let his employees do what they'd been hired to do. Rolland appreciated that he hadn't drawn out matters today.

Twenty-five years of experience, he thought to himself as he looked at Monroe. *Sounds like he's seen and done a lot. I'm sure he has much he can teach me.*

MONROE INITIATED THE CONVERSATION. "DOM TELLS ME YOU HAVE THREE kids. Is that right?"

The soft opener caught Rolland a bit flat-footed. Where Dom had been direct, Monroe was taking a more relaxed, personal approach.

"That's right," Rolland said, catching up to the question. "My daughter's a senior in high school, and we have two younger boys. We're proud of them."

"Is your daughter starting to get antsy about finishing school?" Monroe asked.

"It can definitely get a little crazy," Rolland said, laughing. "Of course, it's not really the end. She's heading to college, so really it's just beginning."

Monroe shifted his weight in his chair, swiveling a bit so he and Rolland could get a fuller look at each other. "I know how that is," he said. "I have a couple of girls of my own, and the elder one is looking into colleges. It's a tricky balance, isn't it? Letting them start making their own decisions and being supportive of those choices while still suggesting what you think the right option is."

Rolland relaxed further. "I hear you. My wife and I have walked that tightrope with Allison. On the plus side, she was offered a scholarship to the school I've been pulling for, so we'll see what happens there."

Rolland was happy to be able to talk about his family; it had a way of clarifying why he needed to make sure he delivered results at work. But he also knew amiable chitchat about home and hearth weren't the reason for Monroe's presence, and sure enough, the consultant moved seamlessly to work topics.

"What were you doing before you joined Arachnid?" he asked.

"I was at a couple of different tech companies, including Novell and 3Com," Rolland said. "3Com is where I got into management. I was in their program, worked with a development coach, and oversaw my own team."

Monroe brightened, leaning forward. "No kidding? I used to be one of the executive coaches at 3Com. What a small world. Back in the early 2000s, I helped them design the platform for their development program."

"I learned a lot there," Rolland said.

"I'm sure you did."

Rolland scanned the room. He realized that Monroe hadn't come equipped with a lot of training material, as he might have expected.

"If you don't mind my asking," Rolland began, and Monroe held out a hand as if to say, *please, go ahead*. "I noticed you have just a blank sheet of paper in front of you. I remember at 3Com, all the coaches carried huge binders full of stuff we'd work on. Have you changed your methods?"

Monroe's easy smile appeared again. "Dom told me you like to get right to it. That's admirable. My agenda is flexible today. I want to hear from you what's going on, and I'll take notes to follow up on things as they come up."

"I understand," Rolland said.

"Let me be clear about a couple of things," Monroe continued. "First, whatever you bring forward, we'll discuss openly. We're partners in this. Second, Dom wants us to work together without interference, and that's why he's stepped out. I'm not here to unearth faults and go running to Dom with them. This is you and me, today and moving forward. OK?"

"Absolutely," Rolland said.

Monroe set down his pen and rocked back in his chair, cupping his hands behind his head. "You didn't tell me about your boys," he said, again catching Rolland off guard.

"I guess I didn't," he stammered. "Well, Rob, the younger one, he's the typical little kid. It's all dinosaurs and superhero movies right now. The older one, Roddy, is a chip off the old block. He just started wrestling."

"You were a wrestler?"

"Oh, man," Rolland said, reveling in the memory. "It was a passion. It's really cool to see the same enthusiasm and promise in your kid that you once had. I work hard for all the reasons I ever did, but part of the reward, now, is being able to be at as many of his competitions as I can."

"Working for life rather than living for work," Monroe said. "It's the only way."

"I'm glad to hear you say that."

"I believe it, Rolland," Monroe said. "In fact, I think you'll see that my methods as a coach and a consultant are entirely geared to making sure the work gets done in an efficient way that allows you to enjoy your time away from Arachnid more fully. That's good for you, and good for the company, too. Are you ready to get started?"

ONCE THE CONVERSATION SHIFTED TO WORK, MONROE WAS ALL BUSINESS. "When I arranged to have this meeting with you, I asked you to email back and tell me your biggest concerns, as well as some historical perspective on them," he told Rolland. "I appreciated your transparency and thoroughness. That makes it easier for me to be as helpful as I need to be."

Rolland remembered the weekend he'd spent laboring on the email to Monroe, how he worried that perhaps he was sharing too much. He was gratified for Monroe's validation of that effort.

"So let's go through this," Monroe continued. "We have Enrique, who's setting himself toward retirement. And Janet, who seems to have some promise but is still a rookie. I'm particularly curious about Brad Graham. It seems like he has been a frequent headache for you. I got some background from Dom, but I'd like to hear more from you."

Rolland had anticipated this. He'd come eager to talk about Brad, because their last interaction had left him wondering whether there were any viable solutions.

"Brad means well and works hard," Rolland said. "It's a question of priorities. Take our new CRM system. He's constantly willing to help implement modules and test the system, which is obviously valuable, but he's here primarily to sell, and we just aren't getting the results. It makes you wonder if he even knows what his job title is."

Rolland smiled ruefully at this, perhaps too sharply worded. Monroe didn't offer any facial response, so Rolland plunged forward.

"It's always the same thing. 'Had another great meeting!' 'We're meeting soon to discuss it.' Always wonderful recaps. Not nearly enough closed sales. I've worked with him and worked with him. I guess that's a big part of why you're here. I'm looking forward to learning your processes and implementing them."

Monroe finished jotting a few notes, then set the pen down again. "I'm flattered that you're open to my advice," he said. "But this is your team, and you're going to have to live with the results of whatever decisions you make. I appreciate the insight on Brad. I have some ideas, and yes, I've worked with employees like Brad before, but I'm here to do this *with* you, not give the answers *to* you. Make sense?"

Rolland nodded. He wished now that he hadn't been so negative where Brad was concerned. It had done a number on his own enthusiasm.

"Let's reframe this," Monroe said. "You have a salesperson who simply doesn't close much business. Despite anything else he might offer, that's what it boils down to. And you feel like you've tried everything from Omaha to Chicago to improve the situation, all to no avail, correct?"

"You could sum it up that way," Rolland said.

"I get the frustration," Monroe said. "Who wouldn't be frustrated? Let me tell you a little bit about an organization in the aerospace industry I've worked with. They had put a large number of people into sales who previously had huge salaries with no variable compensation. When we assessed these folks, we found that increasing their income—as they could through better sales—didn't motivate them. Their salary alone was comfortable enough. They were motivated by helping people. That social motivation alone—helping people—filled their cup. Margin wasn't among their top concerns. Those kinds of results can drive management crazy. Does that sound familiar?"

Rolland had pushed so far forward that much of his torso was now on the table. "That's it exactly. How do I motivate someone who doesn't make a priority of closing? And there are other concerns, too. Take Enrique. He's completely indifferent to entering data into the CRM system, and I feel like that's costing him in terms of keeping contact with older accounts. But the guy is so good at what he does—in fact, we just tag-teamed a big sale—that I can't say much to him. I don't know. Sometimes, I just feel like I'm failing at the management piece of the job."

Monroe smiled again.

"The last thing you are is a failure," he said. "Believe me, I wouldn't be here if Dom felt that way about you. Your efforts with Brad haven't yielded results, and that gets you down. Reaching an older, more knowledgeable salesperson, one more set in his ways like Enrique, that's hard for anybody. But listen. Dom was just in here, telling me how you're a lieutenant and will do anything to succeed. That tells me you have grit. And because you have grit, you don't want to give up on Brad or let down Arachnid as a whole."

Rolland was heartened by the praise, and the ideas that were blooming in his head came barreling out of his mouth. "Maybe I need to give Brad a model of sales success," he said. "Maybe I should go with him and help close some of these opportunities so he can see how to do it. What do you think?"

Monroe considered the question, long enough that Rolland grew a little uncomfortable. At last, Monroe spoke. "Bear with me, Rolland. I like your positive thinking. But let's look at your question from some other angles."

A S MONROE BEGAN DECONSTRUCTING ROLLAND'S SUGGESTION, THE ARACH-nid sales manager knew two things for certain: One, he was going to have to start thinking more deeply about how to approach his challenges; and two, he was thankful someone with Monroe's experience was now in the building.

"Is it possible Brad just isn't the right fit?" Monroe asked. "What I'm hearing you say is that you believe you could better train your salespeople by having them observe you. I think that's a brilliant *first* step of training. But let's focus on Brad. He's been with you a while. If you executed your plan and showed him how to close a sale, based on your experiences with him so far, what do you believe the chances are he will succeed on his own?"

Rolland retreated in his seat. He didn't want to give the answer he now knew. Further, he knew Monroe already had the answer.

Monroe kept going. "The big question on your mind seems to be 'How do I develop employees to the point where they can and will sell?' Do you mind if I share with you a model that has been successful for me and other sales leaders when it comes to teaching and development?"

"Please." Rolland had lost much of his steam, now that it was obvious there was no simple fix where Brad was concerned.

Monroe pushed a piece of paper toward the center of the table, and he leaned in and began a rudimentary illustration.

"Meet the Team Balloon Model," he said. He drew three stacked balloons, one on top of another, and a vertical line on each side of the stack. Above the balloons, he penned a dollar sign.

"These balloons represent a sales team," he went on. "The dollar sign on top is the amount of revenue that team generates and can support. What you want to see, of course, is the balloons getting taller over time to move that revenue bar higher."

Rolland came around the table and sat next to Monroe to get a better look. "I understand."

"Now," Monroe said, "the salespeople in the top balloon, the

Service Balloon, are the top performers who consistently produce high revenue. The ones in the middle, the Partner Balloon, have had success, but they haven't yet hit a home run or haven't shown they can produce consistently."

"And the bottom balloon?" Rolland asked.

Monroe tapped it with his pen. "This is the Assess Balloon. These are the people who are underperforming and can't be depended upon for specific revenue results."

"What are the lines?" Rolland asked. He was getting into the idea. Monroe smiled admiringly.

"Let's call them walls," Monroe said. "One way to raise the overall stack is to fill the balloons with air—meaning more people. But you can also raise revenue by squeezing the walls in, causing the balloons to reshape and become taller. The left wall is accountability. The right wall is Support. To squeeze the balloons, you have to apply equal pressure from each side; otherwise, the balloons just go sideways."

"What do you mean?" Rolland asked.

"Well," Monroe said, "if you push harder on accountability than you do on motivation and development, you come across as a demanding jerk, and that is bad for your team. But if you're too heavy with the coaching and too light with the accountability, you'll be an ineffectual cheerleader; your team will never feel like it has to act on what you say. Understand?"

Rolland nodded.

"All right," Monroe said. "Let's take your situation. You can apply pressure on the two walls. Which of the three balloons should receive the most attention from you? How should that attention differentiate from balloon to balloon?"

Rolland was into it now. "Assess," he said. "The middle-balloon people are producing, and the top balloon is producing a lot. I need to give the bottom people the most help, because they're the drag on the operation, right?"

Monroe took in the answer as if he'd expected it. "Seems logical. Let's take a deeper look, though. Your top performers bring in the most revenue. They don't need a lot of training, but it's worth your time to clear as many mountains out of their way as possible so they can maximize their good work. On the other hand, the Assess Balloon consists of people who need to move—either up to the middle, or out of the company. What do you think differentiates those who move *up* from those who need to be moved *out*?"

Rolland tried again. "Seems like the people who are willing to apply what they've learned are the ones who move up. It's motivation, isn't it?"

"It's precisely that," Monroe said. "Now, another question: Has it ever worked when you've wanted more for an employee than they've wanted for themselves?"

Rolland's clarity was instantaneous. "No."

"So I ask again," Monroe said. "Where should you invest your efforts?"

"With those in the Assess Balloon who show true motivation," Rolland said. "And with the Partner Balloon, so those people who already have had success can experience even more."

"Very good. Now, think about your own team. What balloon do your people go into? And what does that say about how you should approach their development?"

Rolland gathered his thoughts. "Enrique's in the Service Balloon. His results are consistently excellent, and he oversees some of our largest accounts. I need to get him focused on existing clients and closing new deals. But he doesn't need a lot of my one-on-one time. He's an expert.

"Janet has shown she can make quality sales, but the consistency isn't there yet. I think she can be in the Service Balloon, but not without my help. I'd say she's a Partner Balloon person right now.

"As for Brad, much as I'd like him to be in the middle balloon, he's just not. I think he's in the bottom one."

Monroe cut in again. "Let's go back to what you said a little while ago, about getting in the field and showing Brad how to close some sales. Do you think that would be effective?"

"No."

"Why not?"

"Because," Rolland said, "that would be me wanting success for Brad more than he wants it for himself."

"Rolland, my man, you are getting this," Monroe said. "We need to give Brad every opportunity to ask for your help rather than handing it out freely. When people in the Assess Balloon ask for and follow through on help, that's an indicator that movement up is possible. When they don't ask, spending time on them will only steal opportunities from other investments. After an appropriate amount of time, if the low performers aren't taking the initiative to get help, you have to consider moving on from them."

T HE BALLOON MODEL HAD ENGAGED AND ENTHRALLED ROLLAND, RIGHT up to the point that Monroe had talked in such a matter-of-fact way about the possibility of terminating Brad's employment. Brad's ouster had been talked about before, but only in theory. Monroe's directness made it seem much more possible.

Rolland's face darkened, and he decided to push back.

"Even if it comes to that, I can't just let Brad go," he said. "I'm already struggling to find a new hire. Cutting my numbers without a replacement will dig a deeper hole. And have we actually given Brad the opportunity to ask for help? Have I invested everything I can as a manager?"

"I hear you," Monroe said. "These are difficult things. Nobody wants to fire anybody. Let me try to explain my thinking a bit more. What I'm hearing you say is that Brad is dispensable, but not yet because you're not prepared to replace him. But perhaps that's shortsighted."

"In what way?"

"You're a manager," Monroe said. "It's important for you and your team that your perspective is farther out on the horizon. Perhaps you've convinced yourself that Brad is covering territory and might occasionally close a sale. So you commit time and energy to listening to his recaps, but down deep, you've started to tune him out because the stories don't often end with a sale."

Rolland frowned. He was hearing the truth.

"On the other hand," Monroe continued, "you rightly believe that Janet still has a future, so shouldn't she deserve more of your time so that she can achieve top-balloon status? Continuing to invest in Brad is stealing time away from Janet and from other investments that would create a real return for Arachnid. So here's a hard question: Do you care more about Brad, or the entire team?"

Rolland felt gut-punched. He thought Monroe noticed his unease, because the consultant softened his tone.

"The possibility of firing Brad should be upsetting. I don't think I'd want to know you if you got a thrill from doing something like that. But keeping Brad around, I think, is actually playing a major part in why you haven't been successful in hiring a new salesperson. You feel as though he's at least filling a position, so you go to work on all the other fires around you instead of focusing on hiring. You aren't feeling the pain of a void strong enough to want to do something about it. However, if Brad was gone and that spot became the gaping hole you said it would be, then you're going to work harder at bringing in a new salesperson, and making sure that you do it right."

Rolland sat silent and stunned. While it certainly stung to have his thinking so thoroughly exposed, he also admired how Monroe broke down the situation to its core.

"I hadn't thought of it that way before," Rolland said at last. "Every decision I make has an opportunity cost."

"I wonder what else I'm overlooking and what results I'm forgoing. Where else can I reinvest my time? Do you think I should be implementing the observation strategy I thought of with Janet instead? She really does show signs of being a wonderful success here, but she's still green.

She had a tough presentation recently, where the president of the company blindsided her. Then I went with her, and she blew it again, because her ambition caused her to overreach. If we just brush up a few details like how to read a room, then perhaps she'll be able to get right back on the horse."

"I'm glad you're starting to consider these new perspectives," Monroe said. "But let's take it piece by piece. Once Brad is handled and you get a new salesperson brought onto the team, then you'll be in a better position to reevaluate how to allocate your time. But that means you'll have to first address Brad Graham's status. I think it would be valuable for us to make a plan for that and then to discuss proper hiring techniques.

"You have a ton of energy, Rolland, and I want to channel that energy in order to accomplish our goals as efficiently as possible. Think of a bullet being shot from a rifle. Focused, channeled energy aimed specifically at a single target to have the greatest impact. When you aren't focused on prioritized objectives, your energy is dispersed everywhere at once like a shotgun rather than a rifle and you have to hope to hit a target somewhere." Monroe moved his arms upward and outward, miming an expansion. "Do you agree with that?"

Rolland took a moment to collect himself. He wasn't maintaining eye contact anymore and it was clear he was struggling with something. He built himself up, took a deep breath, and then put it out there. "It makes me a little uneasy because I've never had to fire anyone before, but I think you're right."

Now the questions were shooting into Rolland's head. The first out of his mouth was, "What will we do about Brad's customers? I don't want to air Arachnid's problems, but won't it raise concerns?"

Monroe closed his notebook.

"You're being honest with me, Rolland, and I appreciate that," he said. "It's never easy to let your guard down, but I assure you we will make a much better team as long as we're open and honest with each other. That's also a great question. One of many that you have circulating in your head, I imagine. It is an area we will certainly need to devise a plan for together.

"Don't worry too much about it, though. If need be, you could simply tell the customers there's been a change of direction with Brad, and someone else is going to be reassigned to handle their accounts. As long as they are well taken care of and still feel valued, I believe they will understand. Now let's schedule a timeline for next steps to accomplish before we meet again, so we have goals to follow up."

Takeaways

The Sales Manager's New Ally

Mentorship and the Team Balloon Model

THE PURPOSE OF THIS BOOK IS TO GIVE YOU INSIGHTS INTO HOW TO BETTER MANAGE your salespeople through observing Rolland, his team, and their experiences. In most cases, overcoming the key constraint to the effectiveness of the sales organization happens through increasing the quality of sales management, not through replacing salespeople. This is because management has a direct impact on *each* team member, while salespeople individually affect only their own performance.

To lend clarity to the lessons Rolland is learning, we will follow each chapter of the story with a review of the major issues he's dealing with, and the tools and concepts he uses to improve them. These tools and concepts are best practices from the Intentional Sales Management (ISM) system. This book is intended to provide an introduction to ISM, and by the end, you should be able to effectively use many of those best practices. You'll also be equipped to explore them in more depth at the book's Companion Resource website: www.acultureof-predictablesales.com.

In the last chapter, Monroe shared valuable insights with Rolland that can be applied throughout the role of a sales manager. As a coach, Monroe is beginning a mentoring relationship with Rolland, and in so doing is also demonstrating how he would recommend Rolland work with his salespeople. After all, how different is the relationship between coach and manager to that of manager and salesperson?

Most of your responsibilities (planning, coaching, training, maintaining accountability, etc.) to your salespeople rely on a firm foundation of trust. Monroe started by building trust with Rolland. Too often, we sales managers focus on business at hand and neglect to put time into building trust with our salespeople. It begins with showing that you care about them and demonstrating your desire to help them grow in their careers (even if it means that growth will eventually happen outside your team). This focuses on their best interest, not just yours.

> Most of your managerial responsibilities rely on a firm foundation of trust.

Think of being a parent. Instead of living vicariously through our child, we need to look out for their best interests. Monroe referred to this: "It's a tricky balance between being supportive of the choices your child is making and suggesting what you think the 'right' option is for them." To find that balance, invest significant effort and time doing the same with your salespeople.

The **One-on-One Mentoring Meetings** are critical to building that foundation of trust. They should be scheduled at least once a month with each team member. Without trust, what impact can you truly have on how a salesperson works and behaves? You can try to use your authority, but that will often fail whenever the salesperson perceives that you're no longer watching. Trust founded on personal connection is your primary channel to influence a salesperson's independent actions.

Water-cooler chat and storytelling are good ways to begin mentoring meetings because they allow the salesperson to take their mind off their current pressures and get in a more relaxed mood. Monroe opened with a light conversation to start building rapport and to get a feel for how open Rolland was going to be. Trust between two people determines the quality of their future communication. Imagine your best friend. The mutual trust and respect you have allows for a much deeper and authentic conversation than, for example, with a new acquaintance at the gym.

If you have little to no trust built with your salesperson, expect the level of conversation to be limited. However, unlike choosing your friends, your protégé never chose *you* as their mentor. Don't push the boundaries of the trust you've gained. Trust is a currency that must be earned over time.

So, the simple agenda for the Mentoring Meeting is as follows:

» **Casual Opening:** Start with general water-cooler conversation to identify the protégé's degree of openness.
» **Reaffirm Earlier Rungs:** Revalidate that you and your protégé both see the level of relationship and relevant topics in the same way.
» **Work the Current Rung:** Discover what your salesperson needs and wants to learn from you currently. Then explore the topic(s) together and identify relevant experiences.
» **Goals and Next Steps:** Close by identifying what to do next and setting attainable goals.

Remember that as the mentor, you must lead where they want to go. This can be difficult—it depends on you putting their interests ahead of your own, and, for the time of the meeting, making yourself completely vulnerable. To help with this process, ISM provides the Mentorship Ladder with seven progressive rungs.

The Mentorship Ladder

EACH RUNG REPRESENTS INCREASED LEVELS OF TRUST, AND THEREFORE EFfectiveness, in mentorship between you and your protégé. Progressing up the rungs should be approached as if you both were afraid of heights: with each step up taken, you need to allow for some time to let the anxiety settle again before moving on.

The rungs on the mentorship ladder are as follows:

» **Being Understood** – making sure your protégé feels you're listening to them
» **Psychological Positivity** – showing your protégé that you see them as a success
» **Learning The Secrets** – helping your protégé understand what really makes your business thrive as they express interest in it
» **Cultural Awareness** – helping your protégé understand the environment of the company and how to navigate it
» **Career Path** – helping your protégé develop a lifetime career plan
» **Personal Growth** – helping your protégé to see how changes could improve their chances of success
» **Reversing the Role** – accepting mentorship from your protégé

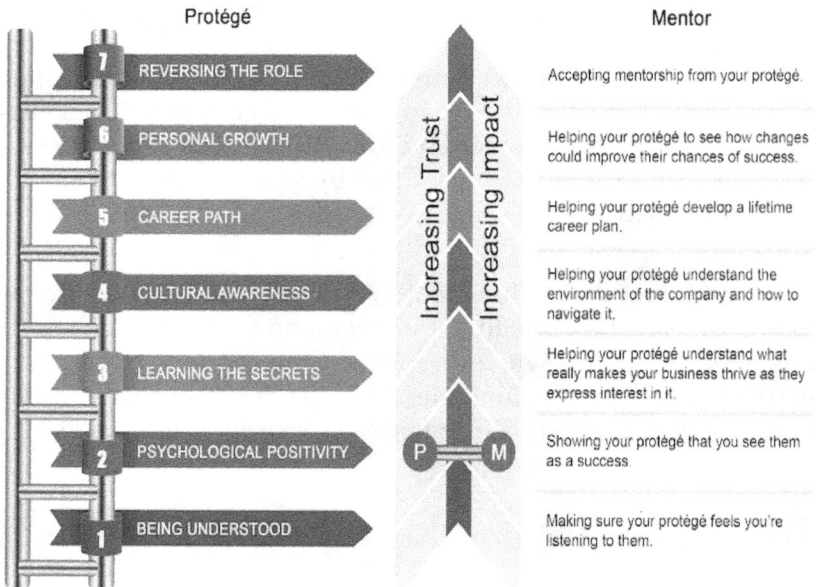

Protégé		Mentor
7 REVERSING THE ROLE		Accepting mentorship from your protégé.
6 PERSONAL GROWTH	Increasing Trust / Increasing Impact	Helping your protégé to see how changes could improve their chances of success.
5 CAREER PATH		Helping your protégé develop a lifetime career plan.
4 CULTURAL AWARENESS		Helping your protégé understand the environment of the company and how to navigate it.
3 LEARNING THE SECRETS		Helping your protégé understand what really makes your business thrive as they express interest in it.
2 PSYCHOLOGICAL POSITIVITY	P — M	Showing your protégé that you see them as a success.
1 BEING UNDERSTOOD		Making sure your protégé feels you're listening to them.

Mentorship Ladder™

Download a full-sized color copy of the Mentorship Ladder by accessing this book's Companion Resource website—www.acultureofpredictablesales.com.

You'll climb this ladder slowly with your protégé, moving from one rung to the next only once you have established enough trust. Don't skip any rungs—that'll just alarm your protégé. For instance, if you had just gotten to the point where they feel they are Being Understood and you jump all the way to attempting to solve a Personal Growth struggle in their life, this would be jarring—and it would likely reverse the progress you had made up the ladder.

The initial rungs can take time to climb and often need to be renewed from one meeting to another. After ascending a rung, whichever one it is, it's good practice to go back to earlier rungs and reinforce the trust- and foundation-building you did earlier. You'll have to do this less often as trust is established but revisiting earlier rungs often in the early stages builds the strongest foundation. You can see in the conversation between Monroe and Rolland an extremely fast-paced example of climbing the ladder's first three rungs: Being Understood, Psychological Positivity and Learning the Secrets. It's not usual to move so fast in real life. Let's discuss these rungs further.

Being Understood means that the protégé needs to believe strongly that you understand them. Do you appreciate where they're coming from? Do you grasp their goals and passions? How important their family is to them?

If they don't feel understood, you won't get much further with mentoring them. Being understood is part of what makes team members feel loyal, connected, and motivated. It's difficult for a person to be successful if they feel like a misfit within an organization. If you want to take someone somewhere, you must first meet them where they are. Monroe laid a foundation of understanding by empathizing with Rolland through his story about his time with the aerospace company. Telling stories to your protégé, especially personal stories that show you're willing to be vulnerable, is a great way to relate through shared experiences. But the best way to do this is to listen with genuine curiosity.

Once you've successfully laid the groundwork for trust, the next rung of the ladder is **Positive Psychology**, where you show your protégé that you see their positives. When your salesperson sees you being supportive and recognizing their positive characteristics, they're more apt to respond in kind. Think about the people in your life who take time to build you up. What's your relationship with them like?

There are countless negatives in every salesperson's day. Your job, as a mentor, is helping them achieve and maintain Psychological Positivity. As you observed, Monroe pumped Rolland full of positivity and optimism about what was going on at Arachnid. He took the critical scenarios Rolland presented, and cast them back to Rolland in a brighter light.

Start developing Positive Psychology by acknowledging your protégé's successes. Then show authentic appreciation for who they are and the work they've done. Directly attribute their successes to a *personal* characteristic you believe they possess. Monroe gave us a great example of these elements when he praised Rolland for his grit. He reminded Rolland that Dom described him as a lieutenant and he reassured him that his determination is not the mindset of a failure. He told Rolland that he possesses a quality that is hard to teach but is paramount to success. Imagine how uplifted you would feel after receiving that sort of genuine praise.

As your conversations develop, your meetings should remain flexible in order to progress as naturally as possible. Monroe was able to navigate to the third rung of the Mentorship Ladder, **Learning the Secrets,** during his meeting with Rolland, but he did so patiently. He avoided succumbing to a serious barrier to mentorship, the Urgent Timeline, which we'll be discussing shortly. It wasn't until he reached Learning the Secrets that he tried to share much insight. That rung is primarily driven through the questions and interests that the protégé expresses.

There are many reasons why things work the way they do, and those reasons may seem like trade "secrets" to some salespeople. And, as sales manager, you are apt to teach such things. But before going there, Monroe ensured that he was at the third rung by asking Rolland, "Do you mind if I share with you...?" This is a common process in Learning the Secrets because it helps ensure that your salesperson is as interested in learning what you have to share as you are in teaching it.

At some points during mentorship, you will almost certainly come up against barriers that impede your efforts to bond or share insights. Over the years, I've seen several of these barriers crop up in multiple mentoring relationships and would recommend that you watch out for the following five gotchas:

» **Judgmentalism** – casting a personal opinion about the wrongness of what your protégé is saying or doing

» **Believing the Lie** – accepting excuses as to why your protégé is limited in one way or another
» **Urgent Timeline** – trying to push along to the next rung of the ladder before the protégé is comfortable
» **Not Being Vulnerable** – causing your protégé to see you on such a high pedestal that they can't relate to you
» **Trying Too Hard** – putting the onus of your protégé's success on your own shoulders when it really should be on theirs

Let's expand a little on judgmentalism, probably the most common barrier to avoid. All of us have a sense in our head when listening to other people about whether they're doing something *the right way*. Judgmentalism happens when we see only what someone is doing through the lens of what is wrong with it, or differently than how we would do it, rather than with a balanced perspective of how parts of what they are doing are actually right. When that happens, the message we deliver doesn't seem to the salesperson to simply offer an alternative solution or to clarify that only *part* of the salesperson's performance was flawed rather than the whole thing.

We simply make a judgment.

It's incredibly difficult to maintain your current level of trust and make judgmental statements at the same time. Helping your protégé discover a better approach for getting the results they want will cause them to desire that improvement for themselves.

Making judgmental statements erodes the trust you've built.

This is imperative because throughout the mentorship process you're looking to build deeper relationships that will enable further growth and development. You're also striving to set and reach longer-term goals with your protégé. Everything you do in mentoring should strengthen your long-term teaming relationship with them. Monroe did so by constantly reassuring Rolland that he understood and was on Rolland's side.

There's another corporate payoff for mentorship, too. A recent study compared the ROE of the list of S&P 500 companies to a list of similarly well-known companies that invest heavily in mentorship strategies like those described in ISM. It concluded that the latter companies performed two and a half times better. Mentorship practices better prepare salespeople for their next opportunities. Their success will inevitably boost your team's success and your company's bottom line.

Mentoring doesn't work if you're lecturing to deaf ears. People engage with questions. Unlike when they're directly being told what to do, people don't feel like an agenda is being forced upon them when they are consulted as part of the process. Monroe modeled this with Rolland when he asked for Rolland's permission to share the Team Balloon Model with him. He was identifying what doors Rolland had opened and was inviting him to walk through.

The Team Balloon Model was a foreign concept to Rolland. He was aware that the members of his sales team were not all on the same level but had never thought about it in a structured fashion.

The Team Balloon Model

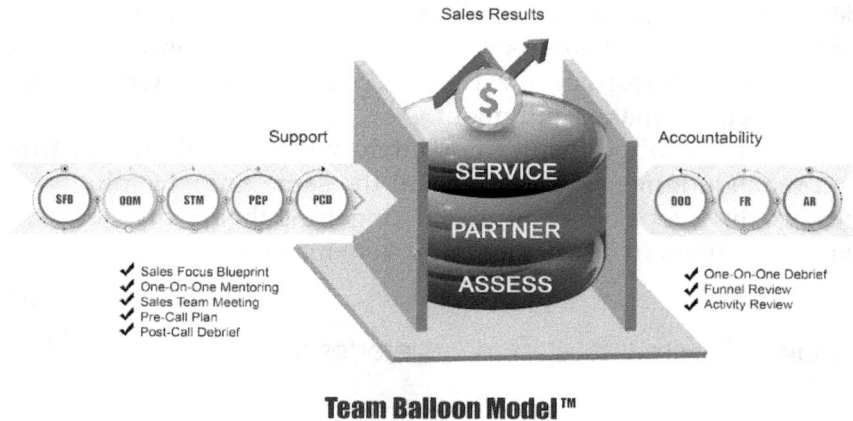

Team Balloon Model™

Download a full-sized color copy of the Team Balloon Model by accessing this book's Companion Resource website—www.acultureofpredictablesales.com.

THE TEAM BALLOON MODEL IS CENTRAL TO ISM. THE FOCUS IS ENABLING your salespeople to experience as much upward mobility as possible. Of course, not all salespeople have the capacity to move as high up as others. You'll recall from Monroe's description that there are three categories that salespeople fall into: Service Balloon, Partner Balloon, and Assess Balloon. The majority of sales-management time should be focused on the middle balloon while also responding to the requests made by those in the bottom balloon, and actively identifying and removing roadblocks that exist for the top balloon. The walls on either side of the balloons, Accountability and Support, enable managers to drive greater results out of their salespeople. When these two walls are applied equally as pressure to the sales team, a predictable rise in productivity and success will occur.

> Your management time is best prioritized toward salespeople in the Partner level balloon.

ROLLAND HAS SEVERAL ISSUES HE WANTED TO TACKLE WITH HIS TEAM, BUT he can't affect them all simultaneously. For that reason, Monroe slows Rolland's ambitious thought train to get him to prioritize.

Brad is in the Assess Balloon at Arachnid. As a result, Rolland should offer his assistance and coaching to Brad, but only if Brad wants it more than Rolland wants it for him. If Brad doesn't ask for help and demonstrate his ability to grow and improve, he may need to be moved out. Either way, Rolland will need to start by making proactive decisions, such as filling the vacant position, for his company.

The Team Balloon Model is a foundation for prioritizing your time as a manager. It helps you identify what kind of energy and effort you should put in with each of your salespeople.

> Mentorship goes much deeper than coaching. Invest in the lives of your sales reps, not just their results.

Mentorship goes much deeper than coaching. It requires that you invest in the lives of your sales reps, not just their results. That means being authentic and vulnerable. Do this, and you and your protégé will climb the Mentorship Ladder together over time.

As I've mentioned, mentorship is a lot like parenting. In parenting, you take a long-term perspective with the future of your children. You make sacrifices so that they benefit. You protect them from harm. You don't impose your own agenda but allow them to grow into their own person. But you still make sure that you're a role model that provides proper influence so they don't have to learn every lesson the hard way. By using these same techniques with your salespeople, you can develop them into being better people beyond just having technical selling skills.

When you invest time and energy in understanding your salespeople, keeping them positive, adjusting how they view the world around them, and developing them personally, you will reap rewards that could not materialize in any other fashion. Having observed hundreds of coaching relationships over the years, including my own, it's been proven that when time isn't afforded for building personal relationships, the rest of your coaching efforts will suffer.

Overview of the Concepts in This Chapter

» **One-on-One Mentoring Meeting Agenda**

- **Casual Opening**: Start with general water-cooler conversation to identify the protégé's degree of openness.
- **Reaffirm Earlier Rungs**: Depending on which rung of the Mentorship Ladder you reached last, quickly go back over the rungs beneath you to reaffirm the meeting's foundation and focus on the goals of the rung you are on.
- **Work the Current Rung**: Discover what your salesperson needs and wants to learn from you at the current rung. Then explore the topic(s) together and identify relevant experiences.
- **Goals and Next Steps**: Close by identifying next steps and setting attainable goals.

» **Mentorship Ladder**

- **Step 1: Being Understood** – making sure your protégé feels you're listening to them
- **Step 2: Psychological Positivity** – showing your protégé that you see them as a success
- **Step 3: Learning the Secrets** – helping your protégé understand what really makes your business thrive as they express interest in it
- **Step 4: Cultural Awareness** – helping your protégé

understand the environment of the company and how to navigate it
- **Step 5: Career Path** – helping your protégé develop a lifetime career plan
- **Step 6: Personal Growth** – helping your protégé to see how changes could improve their chances of success
- **Step 7: Reversing the Role** – accepting mentorship from your protégé

» **Team Balloon Model**

- **Service Balloon:** Identify roadblocks that hinder sales performance
- **Partner Balloon:** Dedicate the most time to coaching and mentoring these salespeople
- **Assess Balloon:** Respond to direct requests for assistance
- Apply pressure with the two walls to encourage upward mobility
  - **Accountability Wall**: helping salespeople hold themselves accountable
  - **Support Wall**: Giving them the energy and tools to be successful

CHAPTER TWO
Rolland Gets Schooled

ROLLAND WATCHED THROUGH HIS OFFICE WINDOW AS BRAD GRAHAM rolled into the parking lot and guided his 2004 Nissan Sentra into its assigned space. Rolland remembered something Brad had said in his job interview about how being able to buy the second-hand Nissan while he was in college had been such a watershed financial transaction in his life, and Rolland had replied, "Do your job well here and you'll be able to relive that feeling with a brand-new car."

Rolland shook his head. In light of recent events, that conversation seemed long ago and far away.

He went back to the document on his computer, an old job ad he was examining. A few moments later, Brad peeked his head into the office. "I'm back from that lunch meeting," he said. "Just want to check in."

"Serbo, right?" Rolland said, looking up. "How's that coming along? Is there anything I can do for you?"

"I've got it moving in the right direction," Brad said. "I did want to ask you about the Rasmussen account, though, since I'll be meeting with them next week about a possible new installation. You had that account before I came aboard, didn't you?"

"Yep."

"The CFO, Gary, I can't really get a read on him. He asks questions, but he doesn't really tip his hand about what he's thinking."

Stone-Faced Gary Garland, Rolland thought. *I know the feeling. It's cool that Brad has slowed down enough to ask for my help on this.*

"He can be a challenge, for sure," Rolland said. "Good guy, though.

The trick, I've found, is to really listen to what he's saying, and to ask follow-up questions. He will eventually show you the direction he's headed in."

"OK," Brad said, "I'll keep plugging away with him. Thanks, Rolland."

Brad ducked out, leaving Rolland stuck halfway in his thoughts about the Rasmussen CFO. *That's progress with Brad,* he thought. *I'm impressed.* He cleared his head, then turned back to his computer and tried to get oriented again. Since Monroe's last visit, Rolland had been focused on recruiting a newcomer to Arachnid. The ad on his screen was one they had put together the last time Arachnid had tried to fill a sales job.

Looking at it now, Rolland didn't like what he saw. The ad described a generic position title, salary, responsibilities, and a brief history of the company. Nothing about it reflected a dynamic opportunity. *I wouldn't answer this ad,* he thought. *I don't know who would.* And, indeed, he remembered that he hadn't found anybody worth pursuing in the scant replies that ad had received.

He sent the posting to Monroe for feedback along with a note:

I don't think this ad is strong enough to attract quality candidates. Do you have any ideas about how to punch it up? I'd like to get a fresh ad out there before the holiday weekend.

After hitting Send on the email, Rolland allowed himself to indulge his anticipation of the upcoming the Fourth of July weekend and the flurry of activity it would bring. The Mandat family planned a park cookout and a fireworks viewing for the actual holiday, and then he and his daughter, Allison, would make a couple of college visits that had been in the works for a while. He knew the days ahead would be significant for his family and for his company.

After a brief respite in which the smell of grilling hot dogs practically teased his nose, Rolland got back to work. He sent several emails to his network to let people know he was looking to hire a new rep. He realized that he hadn't relied too heavily on referrals in the past because sorting through them initially demanded more time. But now, with Monroe's lessons about commitments and priorities fresh in his mind, he wanted to expand his channels of recruitment.

Later in the afternoon, Monroe called.

"Did you get a chance to look over the changes I recommended on that ad?" he asked.

"I did," Rolland said. "I really like the tone of it now."

"What specifically do you like better?"

"It grabs attention," Rolland said. "I like the highlights about employee benefits. And the bullet points about responsibilities sound more like unique opportunities. A go-getter is going to want this job. I know if I saw this ad and was looking for sales work, I'd say, 'That sounds like me.'"

"And that's the point," Monroe said. "It sounds like you've noticed it was written from a sales-and-marketing perspective. That's meant to inspire and create deeper interest in the position. The version you sent me was more of an HR-style recitation of facts. That's pretty common among job postings, of course, because so many of them emanate from an HR perspective. The skill is in saying all the things HR needs to say while also stimulating interest from the kind of person you want for the job."

"I understand that," Rolland said. "I'd say we have the right blend here."

"The important thing," Monroe went on, "is that you noticed the previous ad wasn't quite right and wanted to do something about it. Good for you. You know, at the end of the day there's not a lot of difference between hiring and selling. You have to put the information where your candidates are looking, and you have to stoke curiosity and desire with what you're offering."

Next, Monroe and Rolland discussed techniques for filtering candidates once the applications started to flow in. Monroe set a goal for having interviews scheduled to coincide with his next visit to Arachnid Technologies; that way, he would be present and be able to help conduct them.

"In the meantime," he told Rolland, "I'd like you to do some research and prioritization on the candidates as they develop. Google some of their projects. See what they're doing in social media. That way we can make sure we're bringing only the best in for interviews. Those applications will give you a clearer idea of where you need to dig."

"I'm looking forward to it," Rolland said.

"Excellent," Monroe said, wrapping up the chat. "We have a plan developing. Enjoy your long weekend, Rolland."

ON THE WAY HOME, ROLLAND STOPPED AT A STORE FOR COOKOUT SUP-plies, coming home with a bagful of groceries and a playful tease for Allison, his environmentally conscious, vegan daughter: "Allie, honey, I know how you like your black-bean burgers and all, but I think the rest of us are going to have to stick to meat in order to celebrate America, OK?"

"Do what you have to do, old man," she teased back. A running commentary in the Mandat household was Allison's seemingly quick growing up—"It's like we just sent her off to kindergarten, and now this," Rolland often told his wife. Whenever Rolland started in again about how she was all grown up, Allison was quick to remind him that she'd always be younger than he was.

At the park the next evening, the kids played Cornhole while Rolland and his wife, Audrey, prepared dinner at the grill. Several other families had the same idea for the holiday, and as the day went on, the park's open space quickly filled up, with blankets dotting the landscape like a checkerboard and the parking lot filled to overflowing.

As dusk approached, the Mandats sat to eat—a black-bean burger (no bun) and roasted veggies for Allison; hot dogs, cheeseburgers, baked beans, and macaroni salad for the rest of the family.

"The only thing that would improve this cheeseburger," Rolland said to his wife, "would be a few strips of bacon."

"Yeah!" the boys said in unison.

Audrey Mandat patted her husband's stomach playfully. "You're not gonna starve, big fella."

Just then, with a whistle and a hiss, a bottle rocket flew past Rolland's ear and plowed into the side of the grill. Audrey bolted off the park bench and to her feet. "Oh, no, no, no, no!" she yelled, virtually high-stepping toward the parking lot and the car. The Mandat boys started giggling, and Rolland shot them a look.

"Not funny," he said.

He followed the line of fire and saw three teenage boys, matches in hand and more Fourth of July artillery at their feet. He made a beeline for them.

"Don't even think about setting off another one." He loomed over the boys, and he could see that his physical presence was intimidating them. "There's too many people here. You have two options: take that stuff away or deal with the cops. I'm serious."

"Sorry, mister," one of the boys said sullenly. They picked up their things and left, and Rolland received a smattering of applause as he walked back to his family's picnic spot.

"Come with me," he said to his boys. "Let's get your mother."

After a bit of reassurance and some coaxing, Audrey returned to the park bench and the family resumed dinner. Soon enough, the laughter returned, Rolland's favorite part of family get-to-gethers, and when darkness fell, the sanctioned fireworks began.

"It's been a great day," Rolland said, as his wife nuzzled into him. The kids sat in front of them on a blanket, watching in wonder as colorful lights filled the sky.

O N THE NEXT DAY, WHILE THE REST OF THE FAMILY STAYED BEHIND, ROL-land and Allison set out on their first college visit, a private liberal-arts school she'd had on her list since before she was a junior.

"So it begins," Rolland said. "I know you've been looking forward to this."

"I have," Allison said. "So excited."

"It's a great school," Rolland continued. "Really expensive, though. It's not all about cost of course, but it's a significant factor to consider. The main thing, though, is you being able to see yourself there and how it will be able to set you up for success in the next part of your life." He was proud of his daughter for choosing nursing. *She's going to have a great career*, he thought.

"I understand, Daddy," Allison said. "They do have a great nursing program."

At the school, prospective students headed out in groups of twenty along with tour guides. While Rolland hung back just a bit, knowing this school was probably low on their list given its high tuition and lack of integration within the nursing field. Allison walked up front with the student guide, peppering him with questions, a huge smile on her face. He could see that she was validating the information they would need to make a decision.

"Your daughter?" a man walking in the group asked Rolland as he pointed toward Allison.

Rolland beamed. "Yep."

"That's mine, next to her," the man said, pointing toward a blond-haired girl almost a head shorter than Allison. "My kid wants to know all about the extracurricular stuff. I love her enthusiasm, but we're trying to keep her focused on the academics, too."

Just then, the other man's daughter peeled away from the front of the group and bounced back to where he and Rolland were.

"This is *such* a great place," she told her father. "There's clubs and activities every day, I can study abroad, and…"

"And work toward that degree in speech pathology," the man finished for her.

"I *know*, Dad."

The exchange amused Rolland. He admired the young woman's enthusiasm, but he was also grateful for Allison's focus on the bigger picture.

After the tour ended, Allison kept the tour guide in place as she questioned him, while Rolland chatted briefly with the other man and his daughter. Finally, Rolland had to excuse himself and remind Allison that they'd scheduled a private meeting with a faculty member at the nursing school.

As they walked toward the appointment, Rolland asked, "Are you finding out the things you want to know?"

"I'm learning so much," she said. "I'm glad we're doing this."

"So am I, sweetie," he replied.

Next, they met with a woman who would potentially be Allison's faculty advisor. She provided deep details about student placements, average academic performance, and available resources, like work study. While Rolland took the information as standard, Allison seemed enthralled and eager to please, asking questions of the woman, and subtly but effectively talking up her own credentials.

I raised her right, Rolland thought. *She's doing whatever it takes to make a good first impression.*

They wrapped up at the campus center dining hall for a quick snack.

"No better determinant on a college than the quality of its cookies," Rolland joked to his daughter. "That was the case when I was in school, at least."

"If you say so, old man," she said, nudging him lovingly.

As they drove away, Rolland and Allison chatted about the tour. He tried to put the day in perspective.

"The school certainly had a lot of charm," he said. "At the same time, with that kind of endowment, you'd think their labs would be more up-to-date."

"Did you hear about all those service projects, though?" Allison said. "Dad, they sounded *amazing*. Half a semester abroad for credit, and you get to work with underprivileged kids in school. I looked up some of the pictures from last year, and the looks on those kids' faces was heartbreaking. Being exposed to that and making it better beats any kind of classroom instruction, don't you think?"

"Well," Rolland said, "I'll have to take your word for the pictures, but it obviously would be a huge opportunity. Mostly, sweetheart, I'm just encouraged by how invested you are in this thing. Choosing a college is a big decision. I loved seeing you taking charge and getting involved."

He paused, letting Allison bask in his praise. "And who knows," he said. "Maybe tomorrow will be even better."

AFTER AN OVERNIGHT STAY AT AN EMBASSY SUITES, ROLLAND AND ALLIson set out early on a sunny morning toward a large state school. They swung by Dunkin' Donuts for breakfast sandwiches and coffee, a little caffeine serving as a further wakeup call. As they neared the school, Rolland shared what he'd learned about the nursing program there.

"I want to find out more, of course," he said, "but I hear that the faculty rotates in and out of the field to stay current on best practices and to keep up relationships with hospitals in the region. That could be a real bonus when you're looking for a job. In fact, I read somewhere they're number-three in the state for job placement."

"That's great," she said. "And as far as affordability goes, this will certainly be a great option."

"Now you're talking," Rolland said.

The tour setup was much like the one from a day earlier, with the prospective students divided into groups, led by tour guides.

"The dorms look really updated," Rolland said to his daughter, as they walked past a row of student housing.

"They're nice," Allison said.

"And look," he added, showing her the campus map. "There's a four-lane bowling alley in the student center."

"I'm sure the students here like that," she said.

Rolland found value in the group tours, but he was really looking forward to the breakout sessions scheduled to follow, where there would be a focus on the various majors offered at the school.

When those sessions came, Rolland noted that they weren't one-on-one, as at the smaller college. Small groups met for lecture-style presentations. When the nursing-program presenter mentioned the high rate of job placement, he nudged Allison, and she smiled back at him, nodding. During the presentation on lab technology, internships, and clinical work, Allison occasionally drifted to her cellphone, where she texted friends and scrolled through her social-media feeds. *Two days away from home and her friends*, Rolland thought. *That must feel like forever.*

On the walk back to the car, clear across campus, Rolland tried to draw out his daughter's impressions of what they'd learned. "I guess I heard right," he said. "Did you hear the part about the faculty doing hospital rotations?"

"You couldn't miss it," Allison said with a wry smile.

It was several more minutes of walking, with mostly silence between them, before the car came into view. "I'm ready to go home," Allison said.

Rolland unlocked the doors with the remote. "Are you tired, Allie? I know it's been a long weekend, but you seem a little distant, and I noticed you've been texting your friends. Should we try again with another visit at a better time?"

Allison opened her door, climbing into the car. Rolland followed.

"No, I'm fine," she said once she was in her seat. "I've had fun this weekend. I'm not especially tired."

The exchange confused Rolland. Allison's words weren't aligning with the mood he'd begun sensing from her. His mind flashed on a conversation he'd had with Monroe about uncovering beliefs with salespeople. The situation with Allison wasn't directly comparable, since it didn't concern cold-calling or avoiding particular territories, but Rolland still recognized there must be a deeper reason for her reticence. He recalled Monroe saying that in order to uncover a belief, you sometimes had to relate a given situation to your own past circumstances.

"You seem less excited today than you were yesterday," he said. "Is the reality of going off to college starting to hit? I remember when I was facing the same decision you are. It was definitely overwhelming, because I had the sense that whatever I decided to do was going to impact my future in countless ways. Is something like that weighing on your mind?"

Allison turned in her seat to face him. "Yeah, I mean, it's definitely a big deal," she said. "But I guess I just wasn't as interested today. The tour and opportunities didn't excite me as much, to be honest."

"What part didn't you find stimulating?" he asked.

"Seriously, Dad? That lecture on internships and financial aid was like listening to the world's most boring podcast. 'Here's thirty minutes of white noise. Enjoy!'"

"Huh. I didn't get that at all."

"I'm just saying," she said.

"And I'm trying to understand," Rolland replied. "Can you explain what the differences were between the schools and what you liked and disliked?"

The pep that had been missing from Allison all day returned when she talked about the small liberal-arts college. "Yesterday had all sorts of awesome activities and outlets to experience life and get involved in communities," she said. "Today, it's like everything was all 'magna cum laude' and book smarts and academics and job placement, and blah blah blah. I was bored out of my gourd.

"Don't get me wrong, I understand that I'll be there for an education. But at the same time, I don't want to burn out before I even get to the part where I'm looking for a job. I want *experiences*. Does that make sense, Dad?"

At once, images from the past two days returned to Rolland.

Allison, engaged and active with the tour guide at the small school.

The excitement of the service trips and other activities.

The engagement.

And, then, today, the more subdued atmosphere at the larger school.

The presentations about financial aid and job placement, which had riveted him but not so much her, now that he reflected on them.

The signals had been there. And he'd missed them.

"Honey, yes, I understand," he said at last. "I'm feeling frustrated with myself for not recognizing it before." He smiled at her. "I was tuned into the statistics and focused mostly on what the schools can offer you as you walk out the door *after* graduation."

"I know you were," Allison said.

"But you," he said, a gentle smile crossing his face. "Putting myself in your shoes, I can see that you were talking a holistic look at what they could offer you *while* you're still there."

"Exactly," Allison said. "And remember what you said yesterday, about how a school had to be a good fit for me, not just have the best credentials?"

Rolland hadn't said exactly that, but it was close enough. He realized he and Allison were looking at the same information from different vantage points.

"Right," he said. "There's a lot to take in and sort through. The good news is you don't have to make a decision today. Maybe there are other schools we still need to consider."

"I promise to try to take in your perspective, Dad," Allison said. "I'm glad you're seeing mine."

B ACK AT HOME, ALLISON HAPPILY SHARED DETAILS OF THE COLLEGE TOURS with her mom and brothers.

"Did the dorms look secure?" Audrey asked. "Are there plenty of lights if you're crossing the campus at night? What about the overall security?"

"Mom, Mom, Mom, don't worry," Allison said, reaching out and touching her mother's shoulder. "It was great. Both places, they're like little contained towns all their own, with everything you'd want. One's a lot bigger than the other, of course." She looked to her dad and gave him a wink.

"I just want you safe and happy," Audrey said.

"No worries. I will be."

Even as Rolland enjoyed the banter, his mind wandered back to the conversation with Allison. He was impressed that he'd taken Monroe's techniques on uncovering and made them work in the situation. He'd gone into the tours knowing his own expectations, but he realized he hadn't given enough consideration to Allison's. He understood the bigger picture now. His view was a legitimate one, and he was confident that Allison respected it. But she had additional goals related to sociability and service, and he had to respect those.

That night, as they tucked in, he talked to Audrey about both visits and the exchange he'd had with Allison as they drove home.

"It was really enlightening," he said. "It's like that optical illusion, where you start out and you think you're looking at an old woman, and then, suddenly, the picture seems to flip and you're looking at a young woman. I thought I was hearing all this great information, and it turns out Allison was hearing the same stuff and getting a different message."

"She does have her own sensibilities," Audrey said. "That's how we raised her."

"Right. I'm looking forward to seeing how she processes everything, and how we arrive at an eventual decision. It's just a kick that I'm still learning these things, and she's teaching me."

W HEN ROLLAND RETURNED TO THE OFFICE, PLENTY OF WORK AWAITED him, including the first batch of job applications. Monroe wasn't scheduled to be on-site for another week, but Rolland couldn't wait to share his epiphany. He placed a call and asked if Monroe had time to talk.

Rolland started by sharing an abbreviated version of his conversation with Allison. "It hadn't occurred to me how crucial motivation is in comprehending someone's behavior," he said. "I mean, I understand that behavior can be driven by motivation, but I never thought about how differently each person responds to different motivators. For instance, I'd always wondered why a change in compensation wouldn't have the same impact on every salesperson."

"That's what is called being utilitarian-motivated, Rolland," Monroe said. "Possession of that motivation type is incredibly well-correlated to being successful in sales. But you're right: not everybody is wired that way."

Rolland jumped back in. "That's why I called. I was thinking about my salespeople in the wake of these college visits with Allison. Take Brad, for example. He's clearly not motivated by his compensation. I've been missing the ball on that for far too long."

"If I had to guess," Monroe said, "I'd say Brad is theoretically motivated. When the topic is new systems and educating clients and prospects, he's all in."

"To a fault," Rolland cut in, laughing. "But at least that makes sense now. I don't have to keep beating my head against the wall." Rolland's mind flashed on Brad's inquiry about the Rasmussen CFO. "I'm still hoping his desire to learn more will prompt him to seek out more coaching from me. In fact, he brought up something the other day that I'll need to follow up on."

"Good," Monroe said. "How's everything else going?"

"I've been thinking some about Janet and some recent challenges there."

"Tell me more," Monroe prompted.

"Remember that joint presentation I told you about?" Rolland answered. "The one where she blew it by dropping a figure on the company president that was completely inappropriate for that firm? I've been thinking about that and wondering what happened there, why she went about it that way."

"That's a good question." Monroe paused, seeming to roll the notion around in his head. "My guess: Janet has an individualistic motivation."

"What, like she's in it for herself?"

Monroe chuckled. "Well, when you put it like that…. No, listen, most of the time, that's not a bad motivation style for salespeople. It has to do with wanting to call the shots. It's common among outgoing, ambitious, leader types. I wasn't there, but Janet was probably oriented toward success at that meeting. She wanted to do well. At the same time, she's young and probably feels some pressure to prove herself. She wanted to be in a power position, and she wanted to close that deal."

Rolland was intrigued. All this time, he'd been convinced that Janet had ruined an opportunity with a rookie mistake, and that he needed to watch her more closely until she gained more experience. Now, for the first time, he was considering the possibility that the plan he'd laid out wasn't aligned with her style or her desires.

"I'm looking at it differently now," he told Monroe. "Perhaps telling her I would take the lead as the executive was a miscue. Maybe what I should have done was give her the opportunity to take the lead *within* my plan. That way, I could have brought my experience to bear in the meeting while giving her a prime part in a successful sale."

"That's insightful of you, Rolland," Monroe said. "This is an important breakthrough, especially with our upcoming interviews. Determining a person's motivation drivers early on should be a key factor in evaluating whether he or she is a good fit for your team and Arachnid. I'll see you next week."

Takeaways

Rolland Gets Schooled

Motivation and Uncovering Beliefs

I N THE LAST CHAPTER, WE GOT A GLIMPSE OF ROLLAND'S FAMILY LIFE. THE purpose of this book is to offer tools and systems for improving the way you manage your sales team, but many principles that work for sales management can also be used in your personal life. Likewise, the lessons that we learn while spending time with our families and communities can benefit our professional lives. Rolland proved both sides of this during his weekend away. He noticed differing motivation types while on college visits with his daughter, Allison. He also leveraged some of the tools he had learned from Monroe to uncover Allison's different response to the two colleges they visited.

In our last Takeaways chapter, we learned about the Team Balloon Model and how, as sales managers, we should spend most of our time with the salespeople in the Partner Balloon in order to help them rise up to the Service Balloon.

In coaching, there are some foundational skills that will help you get the best results out of your team. Uncovering your salespeople's driving beliefs and understanding what motivates them are two of those skills. Successful coaching begins with a firm grasp **of** what will encourage them **to** want to accept your advice, and support or resist it.

To follow up further on our Team Balloon Model, let's focus on one of the specific walls: Support—and specifically its Motivation component. Motivation isn't universal. What gets us out of bed in the morning varies from one person to another.

Rolland wasn't instantly aware that a difference in motivation was at the root of the opposite attitudes he and Allison had toward the colleges, but he did observe changes in Allison's behavior. She was enthralled by what the first college had to offer. She admired the community outreach activities and had a strong emotional reaction to the pictures of the travel-abroad service trip.

The reason? Allison is driven by social motivation. Social motivation is an interest in helping others regardless of whether they deserve it. As Allison states, "I understand the value of the education and I know at the end of the day that's what I'm going to college for," but she's not *driven* by that end.

This can sometimes be the case with salespeople too. For instance, if a salesperson is socially motivated, even though they realize that their job responsibility is to close deals and that their livelihood is largely based on commissions, they may primarily be driven by helping people find solutions even if doing so doesn't translate to profits and commissions.

Motivation Types

RESEARCH HAS SHOWN THAT THERE ARE SIX MAJOR SOURCES FROM which people derive their motivation. We've already identified **Social**. There is also:

» **Theoretical**: gaining knowledge especially for knowledge's sake
» **Aesthetic**: putting yourself in position to experience peace and harmony in what's around you
» **Individualistic**: controlling yourself and others so that you have the ability to call the shots
» **Traditional**: having life around you follow patterns of correctness.

The last remaining motivation type has the highest direct correlation with sales performance based on the sales-team assessments I have been involved in. In fact, the primary motivation for over 70 percent of high sales performers is:

> » **Utilitarian**: being motivated by results and seeing the benefits and profitability of those results.

Utilitarian salespeople are the most sought after by sales managers. From the story, we can see how Rolland fits that description. During the first college tour, while he enjoyed watching his daughter participate in the walkabout, the chatter about volunteer and study-abroad opportunities went in one ear and out the other.

But the next day Rolland was far more invested. He was intensely interested as the professor discussed the different financial-aid packages, the modern technology that had just been installed in the labs, the clinical field work that the students participated in at a teaching hospital, and how internships were a graduation requirement.

Being results-driven and having an eye for the finish line bodes well for salespeople. It's easier to motivate salespeople when you can directly adjust their behavior through changes in competition and compensation.

Think about salespeople on your own team, or past teams you've been a part of. Can you associate any of the above motivation types with the salespeople you know? Understanding what specific motivators will drive your salespeople can be a game-changer for your effectiveness as a manager.

> Understanding what specific motivators will drive your salespeople can be a game-changer for your effectiveness as a manager.

From the story, we can link Theoretical motivation with Brad and Individualistic motivation with Janet. Brad loves learning new systems and educating his clients. Janet comes across as young and ambitious, which is due to her motivation to call the shots and prove her talents. Had Rolland been more conscious of what motivated them individually earlier on, he would have been better prepared for handling his team in different situations.

Not all motivational types are advantageous in sales, which means you should look for motivational clues early in the interview.

Many recruiting managers look for characteristics such as outgoingness, being highly personable, etc. All of those are relevant to success but aren't as strongly correlated as Utilitarian motivation. Now, I'm not suggesting that you should *only* hire a candidate if they demonstrate they are Utilitarian-motivated. Rather, you should be aware of what motivates new salespeople before you bring them on so you can adjust your training and accountability practices accordingly.

For example, if salespeople are not Utilitarian-motivated, then compensation will probably not be a significant driver of their behavior, but a chance to develop personally or share their skills.

We will discuss more techniques you can use to hire motivated salespeople in the next chapter. For now, let's talk about what we can do to motivate the teams we already have.

Motivational Techniques

AS SALES MANAGERS, WE NEED TO BE SENSITIVE TO THE FACT THAT THE world in which our sales teams live is one that grinds them down on a daily basis. Salespeople face rejection, get led on by clients who eventually turn them down, receive the brunt of negative reactions from people who simply don't like to be sold to, and much more. These can have a devastating effect on motivation—especially when they all happen in the same day!

> Selling is primarily just a transfer of confidence and enthusiasm, so ensure that you're constantly building up your team.

But you can help. You could set up regularly **triggered celebrations** for certain accomplishments, such as closing a new deal, or renewing an order from an old client. You could identify moments when you can consciously inject positive energy into your salespeople, such as after difficult rejections. You could encourage salespeople to share their successes and discuss the strategy and technique that went into them. After all, selling is primarily just a transfer of confidence and enthusiasm, so ensure that you're constantly building up your team.

Triggered celebrations may seem to effectively be cheerleading. Being rewarded for simply doing what's expected may rub some people the wrong way. But being encouraging and upbeat helps keep your people motivated.

The restaurant chain Long John Silver's has a nautical theme, and many of its locations have a ship's bell by the door. It's there for customers to ring as they exit to indicate that they were pleased with the service and the food. With each ring of the bell, other customers are reassured that the product and service they are about to receive will be of high quality. At the same time the employees receive confirmation that they did a good job. This is a company that identified how they could capture even the smallest gratitude from their customers and communicate it in real time to their employees. This is an excellent example of cheerleading. How are you capturing the smallest amounts of success and growth, and effectively communicating that to your staff?

The **Sales Team Meeting** is another motivational platform. In the ISM System, the Sales Team Meeting is the only core meeting that is recommended to solely focus on motivation. You should hold this meeting weekly to reignite your team's energy and focus toward ongoing goals.

At the beginning of this book, Rolland tried to conduct a sales team meeting. Rolland wanted to bring enough of his own gusto to the meeting in order to get his team equally motivated. He went on to share an exciting accomplishment with the team: He and Enrique had just closed a large deal earlier that day.

A common misuse of the Sales Team Meeting is as an informative debrief session to get everyone on the same page. While the information being shared may be helpful for keeping everyone in the loop, it should be presented positively, and involve all meeting participants. When the focus is not kept motivational, however, your people may feel their time is being wasted. This is not the outcome you want.

More information about how to run an effective (and positive!) Sales Team Meetings will be found after Chapter 5, "An Old Salesman Learns New Tricks."

Your **corporate culture** plays a significant role in team motivation. Culture is infectious. Salespeople are motivated by a team-focused culture when the team is one that they are happy to be a part of.

I saw a talk recently by John Foley, former pilot with the Blue Angels. He spoke about the importance of culture within their group of pilots. Whenever they would do a review of their performance for the day, they would end with the statement, "Glad to be here." That positivity, that strong mental attitude and good vibe around being a part of the team, is infectious. It motivates the others to also strive for excellence even when mistakes are made.

Similarly, you can dictate a positive culture by leading from the front. If your leadership style is perceived as picking at problems without talking about solutions, and taking it public, then you're fostering a culture of negativity. A lot could be said about building a culture, but it starts with leading by example. Be the positive voice in the room, talking about solutions in the same breath as problems. Stay focused on the bright future of the team and how successful the members of the team will be if they continue heading in the right direction.

You should also try to manage the conversations that are happening outside of meetings to make sure that the team is consuming energy and information in a positive way. For example, if you know that the competitor has recently dropped its prices, raise that matter in a constructive way rather than just letting team members talk about it among themselves. Otherwise, there's a good chance that the conversation won't be positive.

FURTHER, YOU CAN INSERT OPPORTUNITIES FOR **TEAM RECREATION**. A HIGHly productive team gets there because they take time to sharpen the saw, and as a manager, part of your job is to make sure your employees take vacations and manage their energy over the course of a year.

If you can send your team to a conference where they will come away refreshed, sharper, and with new ideas after networking with other professionals in the industry, do so. On a smaller scale, you can take your team out after hours for drinks or take off early in the afternoon for a round of miniature golf or bowling. If your team is spread out geographically, you can schedule time to bring them together. Not everyone on the team has the same interests, so vary the recreation from one activity to the next. Obviously, you'll need to minimize downtime, but cultures are hard to build without bringing people together.

While motivation has a strong influence on why people do what they do, the *beliefs* that they have are just as influential. People act according to their beliefs and their habits. Uncovering beliefs was a strategy Rolland attempted to implement in his personal life with Allison. As with each of his salespeople, Rolland recognized that there must be more to the story with Allison and her different reactions to the colleges she visited that she wasn't revealing. Rolland chose to have this conversation with his daughter during their drive home, rather letting the moment pass—and letting his incorrect hypothesis harden into a conclusion.

> People act according to their beliefs and their habits.

Picture yourself having a quick debrief meeting following a ride-along with one of your salespeople, while feelings and impressions are fresh.

Conducting Belief Experiments

SO, WHAT EXACTLY GOES INTO UNCOVERING BELIEFS? ROLLAND HINTED AT the process when he noted Allison's behavior throughout the day and found that his first assumption was off base. Anytime you're trying to understand and appreciate the underlying beliefs of your salespeople, you should start by detecting and trying to diagnose their behavior. This gives you the chance to ask specific, neutral questions that your salesperson can answer.

Rolland observed how Allison's energy level and enthusiasm shifted from day one to day two. As he said, "I know it's been a long weekend with all the running around. I saw you texting a bunch today too." Based on those details, Rolland formed a hypothesis. He asked Allison, "Are you tired, Allie? ... You must miss your friends after a long weekend away." Her response sparked a conversation that forced Rolland to revisit his hypothesis.

To manage your salespeople, you need to be able to recognize trends in their behavior and test your hypothesis about what their behavior suggests by sharing with them what you have observed, and what you think might be causing it. Now "being tired" and "missing your friends" are not deeply held beliefs, but Rolland was at least practicing the techniques involved in uncovering what beliefs were actually changing her behaviors. By doing so, he learned her social motivation and her belief that the experiences she lives are as valuable as the education that she gains. By making a guess at what was causing Allie's behavior, even a wrong one, Rolland was demonstrating that he cared. And that, you may remember, is an important rung early on the Mentoring Ladder.

What are the relevant beliefs that may be plaguing your team? I can think of nearly a dozen commonly held beliefs amongst salespeople that impede their effectiveness. For example, do any of your salespeople believe, "It's not worth my time to put together a sales plan"? Or, "Asking about budget is pushy"? Or, perhaps, "It is rude and inconsiderate to talk to somebody who wasn't expecting my call"? What about, "Best price is the key driver of buying decisions"?

If you ever think you've detected one of these beliefs within your team, it's important to remember that you're merely starting with a hypothesis. That you cannot know, absolutely, what is going on in someone else's head. Uncovering beliefs is similar to the scientific method. Science starts with an observation of behaviors and patterns. You can develop a hypothesis from those observations, but you must run experiments to test what the actual outcomes are.

The hypothesis is correct only if the observed outcomes matched your expected outcomes. Therefore, before you can determine whether a belief is actually driving a behavior, you would start by observing the behavior in the person, and asking questions and conducting experiments to gain more information.

B EYOND SIMPLE OBSERVATION AND ANALYSIS OF BEHAVIOR, ISM PROPOSES three Belief Experiments that you can conduct in order to reveal the underlying belief:

- » Taking the salesperson out of their industry,
- » Reversing the roles, and
- » Relating to personal experience.

Let's look at each of these.

The first experiment is to theoretically **take the salesperson out of their industry**. For instance, if you hypothesize that a salesperson believed it was pushy to inquire about a prospect's budget, you could give them an example from the wedding industry. Get them to imagine being a wedding planner and ask how successful they think they could be if they never nailed down what their client's budget was for the big day. The idea is for them to acknowledge that if a wedding planner knows their client's budget, they are better equipped to serve the needs of the client. It is beneficial for both sides if the wedding planner has that information.

Once that's settled, bring the conversation back to your own industry. Find out why your salesperson thinks that what works for weddings won't work for what they do.

The process for conducting this experiment, and the rest that will follow, is to get the salesperson to state their belief, recognize it is hindering their performance, and accept that a change is necessary in order for them to improve their results.

Maybe the first Belief Experiment isn't drawing out the underlying belief effectively. In that case, you could try the second Belief Experiment, and **reverse the roles** for the salesperson by finding out what they would expect if they were in their client's shoes. Consider another commonly held belief that "My presentations are my most important selling tool."

You can illustrate several scenarios for your salesperson to place themselves into. For instance, hiring an investment advisor who has enough technical knowledge to make you dizzy but never takes the time to understand your personal short- and long-term financial goals, or level of risk aversion.

By flipping them into the buying role and allowing the salesperson to realize what their own expectations are, you can help them see more clearly why "selling by telling" isn't the best approach.

After Rolland discovered his initial assumption about Allison being tired was wrong, he jumped to another ISM Belief Experiment: **relating to personal experience.** He opened up to her by saying, "I remember when I was facing the same decision you are. It was definitely overwhelming, because I had the sense that whatever I decided to do was going to impact my future in countless ways. Is something like that weighing on your mind?"

As we discussed with mentoring, it is incredibly difficult to successfully uncover and replace a belief without first establishing strong relationships with your salespeople. You will struggle to get them to be open and honest with you if you haven't first demonstrated your own vulnerabilities, and that you care about them personally.

Sometimes, relating is necessary because people can be blind to their own reality, or they might subconsciously deny it if they fear their belief is misplaced. Until they recognize a similar circumstance in someone else or hear from someone they trust that it's a justified belief, it may not click. We can see in the dialogue that Rolland and Allison have a close bond. But it's not until Rolland shares a personal story and his own past fears about college, demonstrating his understanding of Allison's ambivalence, that he gets her to let her emotions out and show what is truly on her mind.

In sales, it would feel like an admission of defeat for a salesperson to openly tell their boss that they struggle with making cold calls. It would be easier for them to come forward about it if they first heard that their boss was once uncomfortable with calling people who didn't expect to hear from him as well.

Demonstrating how you've overcome challenges also allows you to outline a process for change that will lead to better results for your salespeople. This sets the foundation for them to apply similar techniques to their own situation once they've identified the belief that is inhibiting their success.

> Sometimes, relating is necessary because people can be blind to their own reality, or they might subconsciously deny it if they fear their belief is misplaced.

With that understanding established, you need to help them discover better, alternative beliefs that will allow them to attain the results they desire. Regularly remind them of the new beliefs that they should be telling themselves to adopt new behavioral habits. The more they're conscious of the differences in their behavior with and without the old/new beliefs, the more they can recognize when they're reverting to old habits. And they'll know what alternate actions they should take instead.

So, if you've discovered their belief is "It's not worth my time to develop a sales plan," the alternate action would be to start each day by outlining a plan. To help them avoid reverting to old habits, perhaps they could post a note on their mirror that asks, *What is my plan for success today?* Keep in mind that change is always challenging and sometimes painful. Give plenty of positive motivation while your salespeople make these changes to encourage and support their progress.

Overview of the Concepts in This Chapter

» **Motivation Types**

- **Utilitarian:** motivated by results and directly seeing the benefits and profitability of those results
- **Social:** helping others regardless of whether they deserve it
- **Theoretical:** gaining knowledge especially for knowledge's sake
- **Aesthetic:** putting yourself in position to experience peace and harmony in what's around you
- **Individualistic:** controlling yourself and others so that you have the ability to call the shots
- **Traditional:** having life around you follow patterns of correctness

» **Motivational Techniques**

- Triggered Celebrations - Cheerleading
- Weekly Sales Team Meeting
- Corporate Culture - Lead by Example
- Team Recreation - Varied

» **Belief Experiments**

- Carefully Observe Behaviors
- Develop Hypothesis About Beliefs
- Test Hypothesis To Gain Mutual Understanding
  - ◦ **Belief Experiment 1:** take the salesperson out of their industry
  - ◦ **Belief Experiment 2:** reverse the roles
  - ◦ **Belief Experiment 3:** relate to your personal experience
    - ▫ Provide Alternative Beliefs/Behaviors
    - ▫ Encourage and Remind

CHAPTER THREE

Adding One for the Team

DRIVING TO WORK, ROLLAND WENT OVER THE GAME PLAN AGAIN IN HIS head. He'd spent the previous evening sifting through the collection of questions Monroe had given him in preparation for a round of candidate interviews. It had been a lot to absorb, and Rolland had gone to bed late, only to wake up early in anticipation of what was coming.

"Professionals prepare," he said to himself, repeating the phrase Monroe had used while telling him a story about how Barbara Walters got herself ready for in-depth TV interviews.

"She develops more than a hundred questions," Monroe had said during one of their phone chats. "She might only get through five or ten of them, but she has them ready to go, should the interview demand them."

"A hundred questions," Rolland now said aloud, impressed all over again by the number. "We won't come close to that, but it's a good example to follow."

At Arachnid, Sarah greeted him cheerfully, tapping the folders she had compiled on the interviewees. "All set," she said.

"Thanks so much, Sarah." Rolland swept up the folders. He was early; Monroe wouldn't be in for a bit, and the first interview wouldn't happen until an hour after that. Seeing Dom in his office, Rolland detoured that way and popped in.

Dom beckoned Rolland to have a seat. The boss tilted back in his own chair, hands clasped behind his head.

"I've seen you buzzing around the office lately," Dom said, a smile playing at his lips. "Monroe must have you running laps."

Rolland could feel the adrenaline surge; he remembered a sort of halfhearted effort the last time he'd tried to expand the sales staff. Now, he was raring to get going.

"Better than laps," he told Dom. "It's like a whole new way of running. I haven't been able to turn off my brain."

"Tell me more."

"The guy just has some interesting takes on different subjects, and that's really expanded my perspective," Rolland said of Monroe. "Yesterday, we had our first interview for this sales-rep job. He took the lead, showed me the ropes, then gave me some homework so I could run point today."

Dom rocked forward in his chair. "I'm pleased to hear that. I had a feeling you two would jell nicely—similar drives for success in both of you. I'd hoped he would stretch you and challenge you, and it sounds like he has."

"Everywhere I go, I end up connecting my situation to something Monroe and I have discussed," Rolland said, nodding. "It's been peaceful to have a more intentional direction, where I'm figuring out how best to optimize my time and give my team what it needs. Now, we just have to find the right person to join us."

"Absolutely," Dom said. "I've never had a doubt that you'd make a success of this new process. Your salespeople are going to reap the benefit of your growth. I tell you what, I'm excited. Excited to get some fresh blood in here, and excited that you and Monroe are setting targets and checking items off the list. That's how we create positive momentum. Great job."

On the walk to his own office, Rolland let the praise and the positivity wash over him. He'd always found Dom's enthusiasm contagious. Arachnid was turning a corner; he could feel it.

ROLLAND AND MONROE HUDDLED BEFORE THE DAY'S FIRST INTERVIEW. Rolland quickly noted that the enthusiasm evident in the office had touched Monroe, too.

"You're in high spirits," Rolland said. "It's great to see you."

"Thanks," Monroe said. "Just got word that my company secured a deal to do some consulting with one of the major banks across town. Looks like I'll be spending more time in Kansas City. How are you, Rolland? How'd the homework go?"

Rolland chuckled. "I about filled my head to capacity last night, and then I didn't get much sleep because I was eager to go. But I'm good. Ready. Just talked to Dom, too, and brought him up to date. He's optimistic about the strides we're making."

"That's encouraging, for sure," Monroe agreed. "Are we still good with the game plan? You lead, and I'll be ready to jump in where there's an opportunity to collaborate."

"That works for me." Rolland motioned down the hall, toward the conference room. "After you, sir."

T HE FIRST CANDIDATE, PHILLIP, STRODE IN. AS ROLLAND AND MONROE stood to greet him, Rolland took note of the candidate's charcoal suit and nervous smile. *These can be tough rooms*, Rolland thought. *Let's start with a soft pitch to get it rolling.*

"Phillip," he began after they all sat down, "do you consider yourself a great time manager?"

"Absolutely!" Gone was the nervousness; Phillip clearly had anticipated a question like this. "I am always conscious of my short-term and long-term objectives, and I stay on top of deadlines as they approach. My past clients never had to worry about receiving deliverables on time."

"Fair enough," Rolland said. He paused, clasping his hands atop the table. "Now tell me, are you a detail-oriented person—someone who dots all the I's and crosses all the T's, or are you more of a big-picture person—a person who creates strategy and direction?"

Phillip weighed the options longer this time. Rolland watched him keenly.

"Well, in general, I believe I'm a well-rounded professional," Phillip said. "I possess the skills to focus in on the details when a task has significant value, but I'm also capable of comprehending the overall vision of a goal when it is presented to the team."

Rolland recognized the politics in the answer, but he maintained stoicism so he didn't tip his hand. He continued on to the next question. "What are the requirements, from your perspective, for a great presentation?"

Phillip sat up tall. He answered promptly, touching his fingertips together as he spoke. "You need to be prepared, have an organized slide deck, have additional information ready for answering questions, dress appropriately, and have enough knowledge to impress your audience."

Rolland nodded, acknowledging the answer. *The words are good,* he thought, *but it's not exactly what I'm looking for.*

Rolland and Monroe both jotted notes throughout the questioning, for later comparison. After a handful of further questions, Rolland knew Phillip wasn't the right candidate and was ready to move on. As per their plan, he looked toward Monroe and signaled him to wrap up the interview.

"Phillip," Monroe said, "if you could identify one factor, what is it that has prevented you from performing better at your current job?"

Phillip seemed to shrink in his seat. He opened his mouth, then closed it. Finally, after a lengthy pause, he said, "That's a really good question. If I had to identify one factor, I would say my old work environment. It wasn't always the most uplifting place; team morale was kind of low. But all of that is behind me now."

Rolland and Monroe stood and thanked Phillip for his time.

"Sarah will let you know about the next steps," Rolland said, seeing Phillip to the door. After the candidate was gone, he returned to the table and huddled again with Monroe.

"Cookie-cutter answers," Rolland said. "He seems like a nice enough guy, easygoing, knowledgeable. But he didn't cite examples from his own work. I didn't see much point in continuing the interview, so I threw it over to you."

"I agree," Monroe said.

"And wow!" Rolland exclaimed. "That was some zinger you threw him at the end. I was thinking that if we were to move forward with him, we'd have to call his references and really dig out some answers about him. Once he answered you, though…"

Monroe nodded. "Phillip was definitely a people-pleasing candidate," he said. "He stayed away from polarizing himself and recited his answers as though he were reading them off of notecards. Notice how he answered your question about being a detail person or one more focused on strategy; he went right down the middle. However, you're correct, he revealed more about himself than he realized with this final answer. He was aiming to please the whole time, so he gave indirect answers and he blamed his lack of performance on his company's environment."

"It was all I could do to keep from cringing," Rolland said.

"Indeed," Monroe replied. "That doesn't bode well for being coachable."

Monroe now threw another changeup. "What did you think about the Question Collection I gave you?"

"There were a bunch of different styles of questions in it, which I liked," Rolland said. "They weren't the typical 'list your strengths and weaknesses' questions. So I tried incorporating questions from each category. However, we still didn't break through too far until you got involved."

"I did notice you were reaching into multiple categories," Monroe said. "That was well done. Those questions are written in a way to tactically adjust the way a candidate thinks. Like you said, they aren't basic strength-and-weakness questions. They can uncover things you want to know about a candidate. This one time I was helping conduct an interview with an insurance company. The candidate had already excelled far in their hiring process so I was mostly there to demonstrate how to use flexible, open-ended questions.

"One of the questions I had included was, 'If I was to contact your best friend and say to them, 'What's one thing John won't tell me in an interview?', what would they say?' The candidate thought about it for a while and said, 'Well, they would probably tell you that I wouldn't want to bring up that I just graduated from an alcohol-rehab program.'"

Rolland shook his head and nearly laughed as Monroe continued. "I never expected as extreme an answer as that. Going into the interview, my understanding was that the company had already drafted an offer letter to extend to this candidate following the interview. I had to keep my reactions to a minimum and continue to empathize and follow-up. In asking how recently he had gotten out of rehab, we further discovered that it was less than a month prior.

"As the interview concluded, I of course left the opening for the hiring manager to take over. However, no offer was extended. After the candidate left, we all stared at each other in disbelief. The insurance company felt they had dodged a bullet. Perhaps down the road the candidate would have been a suitable option again, but not immediately after that kind of traumatic experience."

"That's amazing," Rolland said.

Monroe nodded. "At the same time," he said, "a great deal of the strength in those questions comes from utilizing appropriate follow-up questions. What would you say if, in the next interview, you lead with a question and then I will submit a follow-up before you move on so that we collaborate more?"

"I'll give that a shot. It will probably feel more natural anyway, going back and forth"—Rolland waved his hands between himself and Monroe—"instead of waiting until the end to bring you in. You ready?"

"Let's go," Monroe said.

Rolland buzzed Sarah, and a few moments later a man in his late twenties or early thirties walked in.

"Hello, Thomas," Rolland said. He noted that this candidate was fairly dressed-down compared with Phillip; he wore a blue polo shirt and slacks. It was an appropriate look for a place like Arachnid. He was also fuller of frame, with a well-tended, full beard.

After introductions, Rolland started where he had previously, with the question about time management.

Thomas didn't hesitate. "Yes, I do consider that one of my strengths. It's important to manage your time effectively with all that goes on in sales."

Rolland looked to Monroe, who took the baton swiftly. "That's excellent! So, tell me about the time-management system you use and how it has a daily impact on your success."

Rolland admired Monroe's question. He grinned, and then he looked to Thomas to see how he was taking it. The nonverbal cues were telling; while Thomas managed to stay calm as he considered his answer, his hands clasped and let go several times, and he twiddled his thumbs about.

"I just really focus on staying on top of things," Thomas said.

Rolland made a note: *Vague. No specifics.*

The next question fell to Rolland, and he recycled another one from the earlier interview, asking whether Thomas was detail-oriented or focused on the big picture.

"I think it's helpful to be both," Thomas said.

"Right," Monroe pressed. "But what we want to know is which you are *more* oriented toward. Detail-oriented people catch everything and can be depended on to make sure each nuance has been thought through. But that strength can detract from an ability to see the larger picture. Big-picture people can see the overriding themes of several strategies in order to understand how they integrate and lead to an overall goal."

"I understand," Thomas said.

Monroe kept going. "If you are somewhere in the middle, that would only make you *pretty good* at details and/or *mediocre* at the big picture, or vice versa. Given that, is there one side or another that you lean toward, and can you give us an example that helps us understand your tendency?"

Thomas breathed deep, then exhaled. "I'd say I'm more a big-picture person than focused on the details," he said at last. "But I am aware that I need to shore up my detail work, and I've been doing that. I've seen in the past that it's cost me opportunities."

Rolland tried not to betray his surprise at the answer, writing on his notebook: *Raw honesty.*

"Thomas, in our state there's a lottery ad that says 'You can't win if you don't play,'" Rolland said. "In sales, that might be 'You can't sell if you don't quote.' I've known salespeople who missed out because they didn't get their quotes out early enough. How do you address this in your own sales approach?"

The question had given Rolland a chuckle when he read it the night before. He didn't necessarily believe in that approach, but he wanted to see what Thomas would say.

Thomas squinted. He slightly chewed his lower lip as he considered the question. Rolland and Monroe let the silence hang between them.

"I don't know if that's true, that more quotes mean more deals," Thomas said. "Not always, anyway. I scored a contract last year with a medium-sized graphics firm because I waited. Some of my competitors came in hard with quotes. I made a couple of extra visits to their office and really dug into what they needed, as far as cloud backup and remote capabilities. It showed in the quote I delivered."

Rolland jotted another note to himself: *Impressive and detailed!*

After a few more questions, Monroe wrapped things up, and Rolland told Thomas what to expect as the process moved forward. They said their goodbyes to him, then reconvened with their notes.

"I trust you're grasping the value of the follow-up," Monroe said. "That went much better, didn't it?"

"No doubt about it," Rolland said. "I can see how the secondary questions enhanced the interview. We were really missing that with the first candidate."

"Let's change it up again," Monroe said. "If you're feeling confident enough, I'd like to step back and let you run this next show solo. How about that?"

"I'm up for it," Rolland said. "I'm really excited about this candidate. She comes highly recommended by my friend Joe over at Krystal. Ready?"

Monroe gave a thumbs-up, and Rolland buzzed Sarah to move the next candidate into the conference room.

Diane strolled right in and gave each of them a warm hello and a firm handshake. She even joked, "I hope the others went first because you were saving the best for last." Where the other two had been reluctant at first, waiting to be pulled in, Diane seemed at ease, as if she were ready for a friendly conversation in her own living room.

Once they were all settled, Rolland tried a new opening question: "Diane, when a prospect tells you 'no', what do you do?"

Diane smiled winningly. "That does happen more than we'd like, doesn't it?" She clasped her hands in front of her in a confident way. "If a prospect tells me 'no', my first instinct would be to ask at least one more question about what it is, exactly, they are looking for rather than just taking that as the final answer. The trick is to balance being resilient with being overly pushy."

Rolland nodded. "Can you share a specific example from your past of when you've dealt with this?"

"Sure," she said. "I was trying to land a big client—one of the biggest we'd have at Krystal if I was able to close the deal. They sounded like they were going to go elsewhere, so I just said, simply, 'What is your reservation?' It wasn't them—it was us. They just thought Krystal didn't have enough resources for a firm of their size."

She paused at the memory. Rolland didn't immediately charge in with another question.

"I didn't like that answer, because I'd like to believe anything is possible with my company," Diane continued. "So I said: 'If Krystal can show you how we are able to expand to use subcontractors, would that change your perspective?' I'd built enough trust through the rest of the process that they were willing to let us prove it to them, and we did. Still have the account, too."

Rolland loved the answer and the ready example. He wanted to see how Diane handled some tougher questions.

"I've found in this industry that many customers just don't understand what we can do for them," he said. "How would you handle the fact that most customers you'll talk to don't fully understand your product?"

Diane contemplated the question briefly. "I think if you want to take somebody somewhere you must first meet them where they are. So if we want them to understand our product, we have to start by asking more questions to understand their company and their needs. Then, we can present our product in a meaningful way, which they will comprehend because they can see it being a solution for them."

Rolland had the follow-up at the ready. "In that case, what would you say are the requirements for a great presentation to a customer?"

"Well," Diane said, "as I was suggesting, you should look to impress a customer with how much you understand about their business and needs rather than with how much technical knowledge you possess. So, a great presentation would require that you've brought the correct audience to the room, your presentation material would be based solely on the needs that the customer had previously expressed, and you would end with a clear call to action or list of next steps."

Rolland's mind wandered slightly as he thought, *I'm going to have to thank Joe—he really came through for me.* He quickly snapped back to the interview, though, and progressed the conversation naturally. He and Diane went through a couple of role-playing scenarios, to illustrate possible situations she'd encounter in the field. All the while, Monroe sat to the side, taking notes on both of them:

Rolland's navigating well, questions and follow-ups.
She's sharing stories and philosophies on a personal level.
This is the best interview, by far.

R OLLAND PREPARED TO WIND DOWN THE INTERVIEW.
"Let's say I hired you," he said to Diane. "Tell me about your first thirty days. What would you be doing, and what would those days look like?"

"First," she said, "I hope you do. Early on, even before I start, if possible, I'd be head-down in training manuals and spec sheets, studying up on Arachnid beyond what I've already done. And of course, I want to get out and start meeting clients as soon as possible. But I want to meet them with a good base of knowledge."

"Have you had any formal sales training, Diane?" Rolland asked. "Or have you been learning as you go?"

"Krystal sent me to several off-site trainings," she said. "And I've been shoring that up by taking online programs."

Rolland stood. "Thanks, Diane. I really appreciate your coming in." He offered a handshake that she accepted. "Sarah will have more information for you. We'll be in touch soon."

The room cleared of candidates, Rolland and Monroe talked about how each of the interviews came out.

"You did a great job," Monroe said, "and that last interview showed you've learned a lot. None of the candidates is perfect, of course. Nobody is. But let's see if one of these people is who you need here at Arachnid."

With the recent lesson he'd learned about motivational responses, Rolland tried to keep that in his deliberations. "I liked that Diane said she wants to be meeting clients in her first thirty days," he said. "That's excellent. She seems really driven to succeed."

Monroe stroked his chin. "OK, let's focus on Diane here. Sometimes, even the best of us will fall in love with a candidate before we've considered everything. Let's dig in a little bit together on this candidate."

"OK," Rolland said. "What did you think of her?"

"I think Diane definitely interviewed the best," Monroe answered. "And your point about motivation is important. But think about her answer, because there was a mixed message there. I heard her say she wanted to get in front of clients, but I also heard her say that *first* she wanted to be well-versed and study all of the training manuals. Not to mention her affinity for sales-training seminars and programs."

"You're right," Rolland said. "I think I missed some of those emotions the first time. She might be theoretically motivated." His mind went to Brad, and he thought, *Oh, no, I don't want to go down that road again.*

"It's important to listen for *how* people say what they say and not just *what* they say," Monroe said. "She's a strong candidate. I believe it'd be worth having her take an assessment to confirm her motivation type before assuming our hypothesis is a fact. It will also give us more insight about her sales skills and capabilities, and how well she will fit in with Arachnid. I would also say that her motivation type shouldn't rule her out, either. As long as you're aware of it from the beginning, then you can adapt your training and follow through accordingly. And she did have some concrete examples of solid sales."

Rolland opened his laptop and drafted an email to Sarah to be forwarded to Diane. It invited her back for a follow-up interview and also included a link to an assessment that he was asking her to complete ahead of time. Rolland was eager to hire another salesperson and wanted to keep the process moving quickly, so he requested that the follow-up be scheduled within forty-eight hours. In the meantime, he and Monroe planned to map out a new onboarding process in anticipation of offering Diane a position if the assessment and follow-up panned out.

"It's important that we bring the next person in the right way," Rolland said. "This is going to set the tone for future hires and demonstrate to new salespeople how our team intends to function going forward."

W HEN THE DAY CAME TO MEET WITH DIANE ONCE MORE, ROLLAND AND Monroe reviewed the assessment feedback they had received. In addition to the validation they'd gotten about her motivation type, they were impressed to see the results identified a high aptitude for selling. Her closing skills, in particular, scored incredibly well.

"Thanks for meeting again and finishing the assessment so promptly," Rolland said. "Are you still as excited about the possibility of joining Arachnid?"

"Absolutely," Diane affirmed.

"I'm glad. Today, we just wanted to retake your pulse and discuss what your role and responsibilities could be if you came on board with us." He handed her an original copy of the hiring ad and asked what she liked best about the opportunity.

Diane looked over the ad, rereading each point. She jotted notes along the margin. Rolland was about to break the silence when she finally looked up and said, "It's pretty close to exactly what I'm looking for. I underlined 'Be a leader in the tech industry' and 'Benefit from training that extends beyond the workplace.' These are the characteristics of a job I want to be a part of. And, as I read through the description of who you're looking for, I kept wanting to look up and say, 'That's me.'"

It was everything Rolland wanted to hear.

"Anything that gives you pause?" he asked. "I don't ask this to give you cold feet. I just want to make sure that we work through any hurdles collaboratively. Or perhaps there's something I can let you know that will set your mind at ease."

"There's nothing with Arachnid, per se," she said. "Any new job has some nervousness attached. I just want to know that I'll be supported. You may remember from my résumé that I once managed a hotel. That was eye-opening as far as support, or lack of it. There's a difference between being empowered and being left alone to sink when guests are checking in, there's a water leak on the third floor, the computer system is crashing, and the night auditor quits with no notice. That experience left a mark, for sure."

ROLLAND SMILED. HE APPRECIATED THE HONESTY. "We're a relatively small, family-owned company," he said. "And we're an up-and-comer. At Arachnid, you'll never be left to fend for yourself if you need assistance with something. Also, we've been steadily upgrading our CRM system, which should provide invaluable support when it comes to tracking and monitoring accounts and deadlines."

"I like the sound of that," Diane said.

They chatted a bit more, with Rolland asking more about her passion for sales work.

"I was a college basketball player," she said. "That's been a while ago, obviously, but it still informs how I am, the way I like to really go at my work. I've done different things—I was in the Peace Corps, that hotel job—but when I got into sales about ten years ago, that's when I really found an outlet for my competitive fire. There's nothing like winning, you know?"

"It's the best," Rolland agreed.

He then went over the shape of the package he'd be offering her. He went beyond reviewing her commissions at quota; he drew out exactly what she could earn if she reached the numbers he believed she was capable of making. The longer they talked, the more he felt ready to bring her aboard, and the more he sensed that she wanted the same.

He pushed a piece of paper across the table to her, a summary of everything they'd discussed. "I would like to formally offer you the job, Diane," he said, smiling big.

"I'm happy to join you," she said. "One thing, though, that I didn't want to bring up until we got to this stage. I'd like to give Krystal three weeks' notice. I'm ready for this step, but they've been good to me and I'd like to give them a chance to get my replacement in before I leave them."

"I understand that," Rolland said. "We need you as soon as we can get you, but you're worth the wait. What I'd like to do, though, is have you come in for an hour or so a couple of times a week to go through onboarding materials with me. You mentioned that you want to spend time familiarizing yourself with our products and services, so it would benefit us both to begin those tasks as soon as possible, so you can hit the ground running in three weeks."

"That sounds great to me," Diane said. "How about we start Monday?"

"Monday it is," Rolland said. "Enjoy your weekend. Glad to have you on the team."

Takeaways

Adding One for the Team
Hiring and Onboarding

EVERY MANAGER GETS TO MOLD THEIR OWN TEAM, WHETHER THROUGH hiring new talent or through developing current team members. Just as an artist takes the best clay and molds it into a finished design, when you're Team Sculpting to bring in fresh talent, you want to collect the best candidates, and use onboarding and delegation to fashion them into ready-to-roll additions to your team.

Done right, hiring is an ongoing process. Its perpetual nature complements the Team Balloon Model as well. Recall that there are two walls that you use to apply pressure to the balloons. One is Accountability. Your ability to hold your team accountable is drastically enhanced when you have a steady flow of potential talent that you can access when it's time to sift out the lowest performers in the Assess Balloon.

In addition, you will sometimes lose your best people in the Service Balloon, through no fault of your own. The best salespeople may simply find new opportunities and challenges, move, experience lifestyle changes, or retire, like Uncle Enrique plans to do.

The last thing you want to do is feel cornered and rush into hiring the wrong person just to restore your staffing levels. That's like having a shotgun wedding, which doesn't bode well for longevity.

You should always have a pre-qualified candidate who has gone through most of the Team Sculpting process and is ready and waiting to come on board. So what are the best practices? It's actually similar to a sales process. Let's take a deeper look at how.

The Team Sculpting Process

ISM breaks the Team Sculpting process down into four main stages:

» **Identification**, when you determine exactly what skills and abilities the role requires and attract candidates.
» **Evaluation,** when you screen and interview potential candidates.
» **Recruiting,** when you come to an agreement about the role and work terms with your candidate and get their buy-in for your company culture.
» **Hiring,** when you make the offer and finalize the agreement.

Let's talk about **Identification**. Much like the earliest stage of the sales process, this is a marketing campaign designed to produce leads/candidates for the rest of the Team Sculpting process. What verticals do you utilize to capture leads when selling? Do you use online ads? Do you ask for referrals from within your current network? Those practices are equally effective for identifying candidates.

> Don't force yourself to rush and hire the wrong person just because you have an open territory.

If you look back to the beginning of Chapter 2, you can see Rolland implementing these techniques. He published a hiring ad and made a few calls to people he knew and trusted. His top candidate, Diane, was the result of a personal referral.

> Ads written from a marketing perspective attract the best candidates rather than those just looking for a job.

An important aspect of Identification is to wear your marketing hat. Too many hiring managers make the mistake of writing a job posting as an HR professional would. That means they list the facts of the job: salary, responsibilities, requirements, etc.

But, in sales, when you're attracting someone to buy your product, do you focus on the spec-sheet facts or do you entice potential clients with value and benefits in a way that looks like an opportunity they can't pass up? If you carry that mindset over to the Team Sculpting process, then your job postings will ask questions to draw the reader in and then pose scenarios that make them *want* to work for you.

Diane demonstrated how effective such ads can be when she told Rolland, "As I read through the description of who you're looking for, I kept wanting to look up and say, 'That's me.'" When a hiring ad is written from a marketing perspective, it's more likely to attract the best and most qualified candidates rather than average candidates looking for any job they can get.

This is an example of the tasks and duties description of a hiring ad written from the HR standpoint:

DUTIES (in an ad written from an HR standpoint)

» Maintain constant communication with the VP of Sales to build strategy for future sales growth in the region
» Establish and maintain sales-call plans and report progress via daily call reports
» Manage and coordinate all special events within your region
» Develop/grow existing and new accounts
» Introduce and educate customers on existing, new and limited-time offers
» Review and understand all technical and legal limitations of our products in each industry served
» Responsible for other duties as deemed necessary by the VP of Sales

CONTRAST THAT WITH THE SAME SECTION OF A HIRING AD, RE-WRITTEN from a sales and marketing standpoint:

ESSENTIAL JOB TASKS (in an ad written from a sales and marketing standpoint)

As an Account Manager you will be interacting daily with assigned customers, doing quotations, and acting as an information hub to help them. You will communicate throughout the company to facilitate providing timely solutions and exemplary customer service. You will identify customers' needs and you will use your knowledge and expertise to target product solutions and continue the growth of your assigned accounts. You will be the knowledge center for your customers. You won't just be entering orders—you will be consultatively guiding customers to proven solutions.

NOTICE THAT THE SALES-AND-MARKETING EXAMPLE IS FOCUSED ON THE benefits of the role, and how it connects with the larger organization, rather than a list of tasks and responsibilities. It presents a challenge and an opportunity to be a part of something bigger than yourself, whereas the HR example could be done by a robot if it was programmed correctly. Which would interest you more?

The second stage of the Team Sculpting process is **Evaluation**. Evaluation follows two major steps: Screening and Interviewing. Screening handles the surface-level evaluation to sift through the bulk of potential candidates based on objective criteria, including resume review, phone screens, and assessments. Assessments can also be used later in the process to prepare you for what coaching and development would be needed for a hired candidate.

That's what Rolland and Monroe opted to do with Diane. As Monroe said, they wanted her to "take an assessment to confirm her motivation type before assuming our hypothesis is a fact. It will also give us more insight about what her sales skills and capabilities are and how well she will fit into Arachnid." While they used an assessment as a final-stage qualifier, you can also use them earlier in the hiring process when deciding whether to advance a candidate.

Once you've sorted the best from the rest, Interviewing drills down into the remaining candidates' specific backgrounds, qualifications, and fit. Unlike a phone screen, the interview is not intended to be an equivalent, objective measurement across all candidates. You should have a good idea of what you still need to clarify or discover about an applicant *before* you go into the interview.

This step of Evaluation requires more time because you're tasked with uncovering beliefs, determining if the goals of the candidate are aligned with the goals of the company, learning if the candidate is a good cultural fit, recognizing if they are coachable, and more. To accomplish these objectives, you need to know what in particular you're looking for and then ask *better* questions to uncover that specific information.

To get there, you must be prepared with a tailored set of questions rather than the same cookie-cutter ones with each candidate. Monroe gave Rolland a head start by handing him his ISM Question Collection. It had a variety of questions that enhanced Rolland's interviewing to help determine if the candidates were the proper fit. And, as Rolland pointed out, they go far beyond typical "What is your greatest weakness?" inquiry.

The goal of each type of question is the same: reveal the *truth*. If there's one thing salespeople are good at, it's selling! The idea is to keep them honest as they attempt to sell you on hiring them. Let's take a look at a few of the types of questions Rolland and Monroe incorporated in their rotation.

"**Option A, Option B" questions** are useful when you know there is a spectrum of behavior between the options. For instance, Rolland asked Phillip and Thomas, "Are you a detail-oriented person or a big-picture person?" Along with the question comes an explanation of what each option implies and usually those explanations both sound positive. This frequently causes candidates to choose the middle. But, remember the goal is to reveal the *truth*. You want to get the candidate to polarize themselves, which is done by casting a negative shadow over the middle with the appropriate follow-up questions. As Monroe explained, to be good at both details and big picture, you can't be truly great at either. Another technique to reveal the truth is to ask for a real example the candidate can tell you about in support of their answer.

Open-ended questions can also uncover the reality of a candidate's past. These questions prompt the candidate to share stories and you can often recognize the authenticity of a story based on the details someone shares. Generally, people are better at spinning what they *could* be capable of accomplishing in the future than they are at inserting the right words into their recitation of history. Thomas provided us with a clear sign of spin when he started an answer with, "Well, in general…". Real stories involve details, not overviews.

Real stories involve details, not overviews.

Rolland pulled out an **unexpected question** when he asked Phillip to identify one factor that had prevented him from performing better at his current job. This technique is especially helpful in uncovering belief tendencies, which you'll remember from our Chapter 2 Takeaways. Phillip's reaction suggested that he had no prepared answer. That means his next words would likely be sincere and emotionally driven. Phillip thought he was cleverly deflecting the question to hide any personal shortcomings, but what he actually did was show off his excuse-making tendencies.

Contra questions are another type that emphasizes selling philosophies and beliefs. During Thomas's interview, he was asked the question about how you can't win the state lottery if you don't play. Rolland wanted to know how he related that sentiment to giving quotes out to prospects. Contra questions steer the candidate toward giving the undesired response, and it takes strong conviction to oppose them. Thomas, however, did stick to his beliefs and cited a real example in support. That was a positive point for him. Asking questions in this negative style will often create false negatives, but rarely create a false positive. Be careful with Contra Questions. A candidate can disagree with you at their core, but not enough to disagree with you during an interview. Use these questions only when you're trying to identify the strongest of feelings.

The ISM System's Question Collection also includes **role-playing and scenario-based questions**. When Rolland asked Diane what she would do if a prospect told her "No," he was using a scenario-based question to discover her instinctual selling behavior. Anyone can create a list of questions, but that alone doesn't constitute a great interview. Remember, the idea is to a craft a unique interview for each candidate based on the information you still need to discover about them, and that the real power of almost all questions is in what you ask based on a candidate's responses.

Now let's talk about the third stage of hiring: **Recruiting**. Recruiting is all about getting the candidate to envision working with you.

> Recruiting is all about getting the candidate to envision working with you.

By now the candidate has passed the qualifying stages. They've sold *you* and now it's your job to sell them. Most people make the mistake at this point of jumping right to presenting an offer letter. Isn't this just like salespeople? If a salesperson were to jump straight into submitting a proposal, they would be devaluing their offer. A prospect needs the chance to experience your solution and connect with how it will relieve their pain. Without that, they perceive your solution to just be *okay*, which will count against you when it comes to price negotiations.

The same is true in hiring. What makes your offer better for the candidate than the next opportunity they might come across, or be considering? If they don't appreciate all the benefits and values of working for you, then the only differentiator for you to lean on is salary—and again, you'll lose in terms of price negotiation. Whether you're selling or hiring, rushing the process is an expensive mistake.

During the Recruiting stage, you want to get a sense of what the candidate's expectations are for the job. A best practice at this point is to invite the candidate back for another onsite visit. Rolland did so with Diane and they continued their conversation about key subjects before a formal offer was presented. Rolland stuck to ISM's playbook as he took time to reaffirm Diane's interest in working at Arachnid. He made sure to discuss any lingering concerns she had and, importantly, to alleviate those concerns. He talked about compensation and even used it as tool to further demonstrate greater perceived value when he "drew out exactly what she could earn if she reached the numbers he believed she was capable of making."

One last action in the Recruiting stage is to follow up with the candidate's references to confirm what you've discovered about their past and make sure your expectations are firmly grounded in historical performance. Rolland skipped over this with Diane, however, because of the strong referral from Krystal.

Recruiting can get a bit tricky with candidates who are moving through the Team Sculpting process, but for whom you have no immediate opening. They could get at far as Recruiting while still having several weeks or months before receiving an offer. This means you must communicate to the candidate early in the process that they are merely being recruited for a *potential* opening. If they made it to the end without that knowledge, they would be completely blindsided and likely walk away with a bad taste in their mouths.

Even when a candidate is aware, you still have to play your cards right to maintain their interest. This is a lot like keeping a prospect warm when they've expressed interest but aren't ready to buy. You want to stay first in their mind, but you also don't want to push too hard and risk being overwhelming. You have to reach out in natural ways on a consistent basis. You'll also want to balance the frequency of your outreach with your proximity to an actual closing date.

Hiring date 4-6 months out: Limit your outreach to once a month.

Hiring date 2-3 months out: Reach out bi-weekly

Final Month: Reach out weekly

Once you've got the intervals figured out, the next step is to come up with something new to approach them with each time you want to be in contact. Remember, this all needs to come across naturally, but you want to be enticing at the same time.

Perhaps you'll meet up at a networking event. Maybe you've got a scenario playing out on a deal for which you could ask their advice. That would plant a deeper seed in their mind about working for you since they're being involved an ongoing project. It's also important to make sure that in the midst of your various efforts, you're having an in-person conversation at least once every two to three months.

The last stage is **Hiring** your top candidate. Much like closing a sale, now there is an exchange of commitments via documentation, a handshake, etc. Rolland had an offer letter ready for Diane during her onsite visit, provided she got through the Recruiting stage with no hang-ups. But this meeting was more than a final spot-check. While talking about the benefits and values of working for Arachnid, he was positioning her to want to say "Yes" by the time he presented the offer.

> Start new hires onboarding even before they officially start to ensure they are invested in their decision.

Once you get the candidate to accept and sign your offer, make sure they understand that it will be a tenuous time from that moment until at least a month into working with you. This is when they will probably get more offers from other organizations they have been speaking to. It's crucial that you involve them immediately in onboarding as soon as they accept—even before they start the job. The more that they invest in their decision to work with you, the less likely they will be to turn elsewhere if a bigger number is put in front of them. (Remember what I said about negotiating on price!)

In the last chapter, Rolland made such an effort when he asked Diane, "What I'd like to do, though, is have you come in for an hour or so a couple of times a week to go through onboarding materials with me." He was capitalizing on her Theoretical Motivation because he understood she wanted to be knowledgeable about Arachnid before she got in front of clients.

The Delegation Process

AS THE TEAM SCULPTING PROCESS CONTINUES, IT TRANSITIONS INTO ONboarding. Whether you're onboarding a new hire or you're delegating a new activity to a senior salesperson, the process is the same. Onboarding is one of the bigger management issues I've spoken with business owners about over the years. This is in part because many of us suffer from unconscious competence. We believe that the things we know how to do come to us and to everyone else naturally, and this impedes our ability to break down our skill sets into steps we can teach or explain.

Too often, delegation is treated like an abbreviated version of on-the-job training in which an experienced person shows an inexperienced person an activity they perform and the results they obtain, and then immediately expects the same results. Most people don't learn that way. The opposite issue is micromanaging, which can be just as frustrating an approach for both parties involved.

ISM has an alternative approach. There is a four-step process for Onboarding and Delegation:

>> **Step 1 – Watch Me:** the trainee observes and is taught what they need to accomplish the task.

>> **Step 2 – Cooperate:** the trainee gets hands-on experience implementing pieces of the overall lesson, while the trainer still owns the outputs.

>> **Step 3 – Watch Them:** the trainee takes ownership for the whole process, and the trainer observes and provides feedback after.

>> **Step 4 – Fully Delegate:** the trainer trusts the trainee to accomplish the task with adequate success.

While we didn't observe the first interview that Monroe conducted, he and Rolland went through this process as Monroe delegated the interviewing responsibilities to Rolland. We are told that Rolland watched Monroe during the first interview. (**Watch Me.**) Then, with Phillip and Thomas, Monroe worked closely with Rolland to help him refine his technique. (**Cooperate.**) They also debriefed quickly about Rolland's success between each interview and Monroe provided helpful tips as well as re-demonstrated his follow-up techniques. Finally, when Diane was interviewed, Monroe sat back, watched Rolland (**Watch Them**), and took notes on his proficiency to judge whether Rolland was ready for full delegation. You can access a copy of the ISM Onboarding Form for your own use by accessing this book's Companion Resource website—www.acultureofpredictablesales.com.

> Use guiding questions to help salespeople see their own errors rather than be the bearer of the news.

In the **Watch Me** step, the goal is simply to let the learner watch you, the teacher, do the work. As the teacher you own the results because you're creating the results. What makes this different than most on-the-job training is how well you are able to train by breaking the activity down into manageable steps for the learner.

Once the learner has observed the proper method and taken some time to prepare, you should move into the **Cooperate** stage. You still take ownership of the results during this step, but the learner is getting more involved. The point is to work together, cooperatively. Along the way, you may be performing some activities while they're doing some other activities, and you're cross-checking each other's efforts. This allows the learner to master individual aspects of an activity before trying to combine them all and complete the full activity on their own—which is the end goal of the Cooperate step.

When you move to **Watch Them**, ownership of the results changes. While watching them, communicate to the learner that they are responsible for the outcome. The key rule at this stage, and the one that's hardest to follow, is that you are not allowed to save them unless the results would be absolutely unbearable. Monroe communicated clearly to Rolland, "If you're feeling confident enough, I'd like to step back and let you to run this next show solo." In that situation, the learner was aware and willing to take ownership of the activity, and both he and the teacher understood their roles.

Not all Watch Them steps are seamless. If and when your learner stumbles, you'll want to review their performance with them. But make sure to use guiding questions to allow them to identify their error on their own, rather than give them the details up front. Once you've reached the point where you're confident the learner will perform up to, or beyond, your expectations, you can sign off on the activity and **Fully Delegate** it to them.

Up until this step, you will have only been signing off on individual aspects of, or steps within, an activity. Now you are entrusting them to consistently produce results that will reflect well on your company. Always remember that even Fully Delegated activities should periodically be observed. Every now and then, just ensure that you are getting what you expect.

Overview of the Concepts in This Chapter

For your review, here are the primary best practices covered in this chapter:

» **The Team Sculpting Process**

- **Stage 1 – Identification:** finding candidates who could potentially "buy what you're selling" and getting them to raise their hand to demonstrate personal interest

- **Stage 2 – Evaluation:** a qualification process to ensure that the candidate is someone who you have a strong interest in hiring
  - ○ Screening
  - ○ Interviewing
- **Stage 3 – Recruiting:** the selling process of coming to an agreement on terms, job responsibilities, and cultural buy-in
- **Stage 4 – Hiring:** final negotiations and agreement of an offer letter

» **Onboarding and Delegating**

- **Step 1 – Watch Me:** the trainee observes and is taught all of the knowledge needed to be able to accomplish the task.
- **Step 2 – Cooperate:** the trainee gets hands-on experience implementing pieces of the overall lesson, while the trainer still owns the outputs.
- **Step 3 – Watch Them:** the trainee takes ownership for the whole process, top to bottom, and the trainer observes and provides feedback after.
- **Step 4 – Fully Delegate:** the trainer trusts the trainee to accomplish the task with adequate success.

CHAPTER FOUR
The Boss Lays It on the Line

Sunday came around, and the distinct scent of spices filled the air at Dom's house. Cumin and cayenne pepper, cilantro and ancho chili. The wafting, beguiling, effusive aroma of *arroz con pollo*. Rare was the Sunday that didn't find the Diaz home filled to overflowing with family—Dom and Estella and their two daughters; Carlos and his wife; Uncle Enrique; and others.

Carlos and his wife, Pilar, had arrived first, with Pilar making a beeline to the kitchen to assist in preparations. Carlos said hi to the girls and then posted up at the bowl of chips and black-bean salsa. Next through the door was Enrique. The Diaz girls bolted from the couch and tackled him in the hallway, with Enrique feigning submission. Dom trotted over, rescuing him.

"OK, OK, girls, leave some of Uncle Enrique for the rest of us," Dom said. Enrique stood and dusted himself off, and he and his nephew grinned at each other. Dom handed Enrique his favorite *cerveza*, and with a wave to Carlos, Enrique headed out the door to the backyard to sit in the sun and enjoy his drink.

Dom, shaking his head and laughing, joined Carlos at the table. For a moment, it was just the two brothers.

"Hey, I've been meaning to ask how things are going with Rolland and the consultant," Carlos said. "Sorry, I forget his name."

"Monroe," Dom said. "I'm hearing and seeing good things."

"Right, Monroe. I only ask because it seems like the tech team has had more unscheduled open time than usual."

"Oh?" Dom asked.

"Yeah, it's down a little bit. Just wanted to check. Maybe it's an aberration."

Dom sipped his lemonade. "I don't know, Carlos. My mind has been so focused on the expansion to Spring—"

"Does anyone know if Marcus is coming?" Estella shouted from the kitchen.

"No!" came the shouts from three directions—Dom and Carlos at the table, the Diaz girls in the living room, and Enrique on the patio.

"Strange that he hasn't been here the past few weeks," Dom said to Carlos.

"I think he's seeing someone," Carlos said of Marcus, the youngest of his and Dom's cousins, and a sales engineer at Arachnid. "I don't know for sure. You know Marcus. He keeps personal things pretty close to the vest, especially at work."

"Yes. Yes, he does."

Carlos rounded back to the previous topic. "Look, I'm not wanting to cause trouble for anybody, Dom, but I think it'd be good if you checked into this slowdown a little closer. You're the one we rely on to keep the ship headed in the right direction, you know? I'm just saying."

"I understand," Dom said. "You know, we're in the midst of change here, and that's a process everyone has to contribute to. But you're right, OK? The overall direction lies with me. I'll look into it."

Estella came into the dining room from the kitchen, carrying a massive platter of food. "Come eat."

The family members flurried around the table, finding their seats. Heads bowed, they listened as Enrique said grace. Serving dishes rotated around, plates got piled high with food, and laughter abounded.

Through it all, Dom smiled but said little. He picked at his food.

Estella leaned in. "You OK, honey?"

Dom clasped her hand. "Just a little preoccupied, I guess. Dinner is delicious. You've outdone yourself again."

"What are we having next week?" Carlos asked.

"I nominate Pilar's *enchiladas suizas*," Estella said.

"You're on," Pilar replied.

Dom ate a bite of food. It really *was* wonderful, of course, but he found his thoughts being pulled away from family time.

Carlos wouldn't have said anything if he wasn't concerned, he thought. *I know we're making some long-term progress—I can see it in the way Rolland's so engaged in his work. But we're expanding, and we can't have a slump. Not now.*

He looked to his wife, who'd orchestrated everything today. She was the center of the family, the force of gravity that kept everything in alignment.

A business is like Sunday dinner, he thought now. *You're waiting for the meal, but you need some chips and salsa to keep everybody satisfied until dinner is served. I need to see some short-term effort while we're in pursuit of bigger things.*

THE NEXT DAY BROUGHT A SENSE OF ANTICIPATION AT ARACHNID. DIANE, after a few weeks of onboarding checkpoints, officially joined the team. The sales team, in particular, felt as though a corner had been turned. After a brief, friendly chat with Diane, Dom headed over to Monroe, who was back in town for an on-site visit.

"Can we chat in my office?" Dom asked.

"Certainly."

They walked down the hallway together. Once they were settled in, Dom moved to the issue that had been giving him heartburn all morning.

"I'm excited about the progress you and Rolland are making," Dom said. "I want to say that first. And it's great that Diane is now aboard, because she seems like a real go-getter. At the same time, though, that increases our expenses here while we're in the middle of expanding to Springfield."

"I understand," Monroe said.

"I've been looking at the numbers from both locations," Dom went on. "Sales have dropped ten percent year over year for the past two months. Look, I know it takes a while for what you and Rolland are working on to bear fruit, but this is an unsustainable number. If we don't turn it around fast, there won't be enough funding for the expansion. What can you and Rolland do over the next few weeks to get the numbers up? We can't bleed like this."

Monroe leaned forward. "You cited increased expenses as a specific concern," he said. "Do you think it's time for us to part ways with Brad?"

"I—" Dom ended the thought abruptly. He looked to the ceiling, then back at Monroe. "I don't know. On one hand, it would be great to have that payroll back in our pockets. But you and I were just out there—it's exciting. You can feel it. I'd hate to flip that atmosphere upside down. I know how important momentum is. You said it yourself: sales is nothing more than a transfer of confidence and enthusiasm."

"Indeed," Monroe said.

"Brad isn't producing the most, but people like him," Dom continued. "Honestly, I'm more focused on increasing revenue than decreasing costs. We need to kick-start the team again in another way."

"OK," Monroe began.

"I will tell you this," Dom cut back in. "I think the CRM system is done. Brad doesn't need to spend another minute tinkering with it. He can focus his energy on selling now. In fact, we've had this system at some stage of implementation for quite some time. It seems to me that we now ought to be using it to hold people accountable for bringing immediate action in the short term."

"Agreed," Monroe said.

"I want to see the excitement out there in the office"—Dom waved his hand toward the door—"turned into energy in the field. We should be making sales out there rather than sitting in here high-fiving each other."

He looked to Monroe, giving him the floor. Dom was a little frustrated with himself for ranting, but he knew the peril if the slump continued.

"Dom," Monroe said, "I appreciate your concern. I think there are a number of things we can and will do to turn this around quickly. I just want to make sure we don't give up on building the foundation correctly just so we can hit some short-term success. I'm sure you agree."

"You're right, I do," Dom said. "I trust your process, but the numbers don't lie. Get with Rolland and figure this out, then let's have another meeting to discuss the plan as soon as possible."

D OM'S URGENCY SUCCESSFULLY TRANSFERRED, MONROE LEFT THE OFFICE in search of Rolland. He found the Arachnid sales manager getting a hallway briefing from Enrique.

"I'm sorry to interrupt, guys," Monroe said. "Rolland, I need a quick word in your office now."

"We'll have to catch up later," Rolland said to Enrique.

They made a direct line to Rolland's office, with Rolland giving a quick nod to Sarah as they passed. Once they were situated, Rolland asked, "What's up?"

"As it turns out, I've got bad news and bad news," Monroe said.

Rolland swallowed hard. "Oh, no. What is it?"

"I just talked to Dom," Monroe said. "We've got a couple of months of slumping sales that need fixing, and fast. He's still excited about what we're doing, but he made it clear that he needs to see some faster turnaround on sales. He asked me what we could do to get more sales in here in the next few weeks. You and I have some planning to do, because he wants to hear from us tomorrow."

"OK," Rolland said. "You said bad news and bad news. Anything else?"

"Yep. I've had a European vacation scheduled for months. I leave the day after tomorrow. So whatever we come up with, you're going to have to execute on your own while I'm away."

"I see."

"Hey, look," Monroe said. "The phones work in Europe, too. If you really need me, we can talk. But time is of the essence, obviously."

Monroe went on, sharing Dom's thoughts and concerns, as well as his sharp words about using the CRM system to hold the sales team's feet to the fire.

"That's a great idea for Brad," Rolland chimed in. "He made the CRM his pet project. It would be poetic if we used it to hold him accountable."

"I think you're on the right track," Monroe said. "But let me ask you something, Rolland: what, exactly, does 'accountable' mean to you?"

"It means that when you have a quota, you're on track and you've got more sales in the funnel to work on once your current deals close."

"That would be a great step toward accountability," Monroe agreed. "Here's another question: how long does it take for sales to close around here?"

Rolland thought for a moment. "Roughly, I'd say three to six weeks," he said. "Of course, there are also those that take as long as six months."

Monroe zeroed in. "Let's talk about Brad. If you start today looking at his closed deals and those that are in his funnel, how far would he be from his quota?"

Rolland shook his head. "It'd be a significant gap."

"How many of the deals in his funnel would Brad say are on the verge of closing?" Monroe asked.

Rolland now rolled his eyes. "Too many. Brad has this way of stuffing his funnel without understanding how far along each deal is or how realistic the chances are that the deals will close in his favor. He believes every open deal is going to close successfully. 'Yeah, I've got sales coming, don't worry.' That's what I hear from Brad."

Monroe posed another hypothetical. "If Brad started documenting more granularly what he believes about his deals, would that help you increase sales over the next several weeks?"

"No," Rolland conceded.

"Or would it, perhaps, help shed a light on what changes the two of you would have to make in order to get him on track with his goals?" Monroe now asked.

"Documentation alone, probably not," Rolland said.

"So other than increasing the level of documentation, how would it be holding him to account?" Monroe asked.

Rolland grimaced. "I see your point. So what do we do?"

"Good question," Monroe said. "If your life depended on it, what would you have to do with Brad in order to get more revenue from him in a short time?"

"I'd have him document everything he knows about each of his deals so we could discuss them in detail," Rolland said. "Then, I'd pick the ones I felt had the best chance of coming through and take on the responsibility of co-selling them."

"All right," Monroe said. "Taking the weight on your own shoulders does seem like an approach you'd go for. My second question is this: If you needed to change one or two things about Brad so he would be more effective in the future, what would those things be?"

Rolland chuckled. "How long do you have?" Monroe didn't laugh. *He wants priority items, not an exhaustive list.* "I'd hold him accountable to asking better questions of his customers during the Discovery phase and being able to document and support BANTC," Rolland said, rattling off the initials for Budget, Authority, Needs, Timeframe, and Credibility. "Then, I would make sure he's holding the right amount of face-to-face appointments with the appropriate decision-makers. If he gets out in front of the customers more and has focused, productive conversations while he's there, I believe he would be more in touch with his sales and better able to affect his outcomes."

"That's very good," Monroe said, nodding. "Now, how could you measure whether he was or wasn't following through?"

"I'd need to ensure that his face-to-face appointments were of high quality and that he wasn't exiting the Discovery stage prematurely."

"Perfect," Monroe said. "It sounds like you need to identify which deals you want to go work alongside him. And you need to measure proper Discovery conversations and face-to-face meetings through the CRM system. Does this seem like a better approach than waiting for the final results without indicators along the way?"

"It does," Rolland agreed.

"You know," Monroe said, "last year, I faced a similar situation with my daughter. She'd just gone through a pretty bad breakup—typical teenage stuff, I think, but it really threw her for a loop. My wife and I really struggled to get her focused again on school. You know, she was spending too much time on her phone, playing games or Snapchat, or whatever. I kept telling her, 'If you don't spend enough time on your schoolwork, you're going to fall behind, and then it's going to be a struggle to get out of that rut.' And she'd say, 'It's fine. I've got this. Just wait until my report card comes in.'"

"Sounds like Brad," Rolland popped in.

"Exactly! So, anyway, my wife and I were nervous, but we took her word for it, because she insisted all was fine. The quarter ends, the report card shows up, and our fears were realized. It was a pitiful performance, and we couldn't help but feel partially responsible since we hadn't been prudent enough in checking her actual progress along the way. We knew better, but we waited for the final results. We could've gotten out in front of the problem had we taken the approach that you're suggesting you take with Brad."

Monroe clasped his hands and jutted the fused index fingers toward Rolland. "If you know what's required in the middle of a sale in order to realize a close in the end, then those are the activities you need to hold Brad accountable to," he said. "If in most cases, sales that close require complete understanding of BANTC and at least a couple of face-to-face meetings, then holding Brad account-able to those activities will increase the likelihood that he closes more sales."

"This makes sense," Rolland said. "I know I can have Brad enter his individual activities into the CRM system as he completes them. Now I just have to set the standards and regular review times for BANTC Discovery and face-to-face meetings with deci-sion-makers."

"Precisely," Monroe confirmed. "Not only that, but you'll get a better feel for his motivation level. You'll be able to tell whether he's improving his output or whether you need to consider more dras-tic consequences for any shortcomings. If Brad can deliver on the level of activities you both agree to, then the sales should eventu-ally come. What's important is that Brad understands exactly what is expected of him and that there is a clear scoreboard for you and him to both monitor his progress so there is no question of where he stands."

"As long as I'm going to be setting individual goals for Brad and defining quantitative expectations, does it make sense to reward him somehow if he proves to be successful?" Rolland asked.

"Absolutely," Monroe said. "Any time you're practicing accountability, you should look to reward accomplishments. It's the old saying about catching more flies with honey than vinegar. If you want your salespeople to repeat their successes, then you should reward them rather than only delivering consequences for shortcomings, which makes you come across as a jerk. Dom men-tioned it this morning, how much he appreciates sustaining posi-tive motivation in the midst of our process. So we need to make sure that while we're holding team members accountable, we do so in a positive manner."

"Understood," Rolland said.

"On a separate note," Monroe added, "I don't think Brad should be the sole participant. He can definitely be the poster child for showing off the CRM system, since that's where his interests lie, but he's not alone in needing some accountability measures. Janet, for instance. She shows promise, but do you believe she comes into work each day with a set game plan?"

"No, I suppose not," Rolland conceded. "But, I don't think that means she needs to be put on a remedial plan, either. She's had some good sales coming in."

"Who said anything about a remedial plan?"

"Well, when you start measuring how many face-to-face meetings a salesperson has, that seems like a remedial plan to me," Rolland said.

"This is interesting." Monroe rocked back in his chair. "If you're of the impression that accountability is a remedial plan, then you'll probably suggest as much to your salespeople when you sit down with them. When we talk about accountability, I want you think of it as a partnership, not a punishment. Not only are we going to incorporate a reward at the end, like you suggested, but the real foundation for the program is that you're supporting them in their effort to reach the goals *they* want to accomplish."

"I see," Rolland said.

Monroe went on. "Remember when I was talking about my daughter?"

"Sure."

"I wasn't looking to track her hours of doing homework each night just as supervision. My reasoning had to do with her best interest when it came to final grades. Janna wanted to go to an Ivy League school—that had been her goal since she was in junior high. I knew what her aspirations were and I wanted to help her reach them. The same goes for your salespeople. Janet is in your Partner balloon. That means together you both need to identify her long-term goals and help her connect the dots to the sales actions that will allow her to reach them. And by long-term goals, I mean the things that will leave her upset if she doesn't get there."

Rolland nodded as Monroe went on.

"For example, everyone has a dream of a new house, or a boat, or car, or something like that," Monroe said. "But, when they don't *really* expect to get it, it doesn't actually impact their behavior. When they believe it is imperative for them to make a certain amount, then there's no limit on what they'll do in order to get there. As a coach and mentor, you should have a solid understanding of her personal motivations. That also takes some burden off you because instead of holding a stick, you'll simply be reminding her of her own goals. We want to create a plan that ends with the income she believes she should make and backs all the way up into the behaviors and activities necessary to reaching her personal expectations. Letting her set the endgame is far more motivating than enacting a remedial sales plan."

Clarity washed over Rolland.

"So while we are monitoring her outputs, the plan will be designed more in a way that emphasizes coaching and growth than it does consequences." Rolland paused, letting the full realization of it settle in. "Not to mention, if I get both of them onboard with some personal accountabilities, I can introduce more of an office-wide reward program as opposed to individual perks. Salespeople are competitive; they won't want to let any of the others beat them."

"No doubt about that," Monroe agreed with a laugh. "Let's get back to Janet: I think it's important that you help her create a written plan. Not just for a week, but month-to-month and even over the next year. You want to get her thinking about her entire sales process and let her determine the ratios that she's comfortable with reaching. Of course, as a coach—and, most important, a *partner*—you can share your insights and experience about realistic ratios and what level of activities will actually result in making sales."

"Absolutely," Rolland said.

"The reason for having the plan written down is because she's in your middle balloon, so you and she need to be on the same page in order to work together toward her goals," Monroe said. "Having Janet write down those goals—and this is the biggie, *sharing* them with you—will make her incredibly more likely to follow through. She's worth the investment to work closely with and really make this program have a strong impact on her growth."

"Right," Rolland said. He picked up the ball with regard to Brad. "And since Brad is in the Assess Balloon, with him maybe I can just focus on the handful of areas I pointed out before and assess his performance accordingly."

"That's it," Monroe said. "If he picks up the ball from there and improves himself, then you could consider spending the effort and time in putting together a larger-scale plan with him as well."

"I can do that," Rolland said. "I'm really excited to begin. I'm sure this will get the ball rolling."

Monroe then spent some time teaching Rolland the ISM process for rolling out a complete territory plan. Rolland was engaged, asking questions where necessary. He mentioned again how happy he was to be learning something he could put into practice with the team.

"I'm pleased with your sense of urgency," Monroe told Rolland. "I trust you can see the benefits of planning and setting up your team for success."

"Absolutely," Rolland replied. "We're going to be plenty busy while you're away."

"No doubt," Monroe said. "But I'm not gone yet. Let's make sure we sit down with Dom first thing tomorrow."

T HE NEXT MORNING, AT BREAKFAST, AUDREY NODDED TO ROLLAND. "The red tie," she said. "I like it."

"Trying to project a little power," Rolland said, smiling. "Big meeting with Dom. We need to show him we can overcome this slump."

"Are you worried?" Her face expressed concern.

"A little," he said. "But we'll get there."

Rolland put his dishes in the sink, then went to brush his teeth and grab his phone. A few minutes later, when Audrey saw him to the door, she adjusted his tie. "Red becomes you," she said. "You've got this."

B Y CHANCE, ROLLAND AND MONROE MET IN THE PARKING LOT AT ARACHNID. "Morning," Rolland said. "You ready for this?"

"Sure am," Monroe said. "We have a good plan. He'll recognize that."

"Vacation coming up for you," Rolland said, winking.

"I'm a hundred percent here, don't worry." Monroe then chuckled. "But, yeah. It's been a long time coming."

Inside, Dom asked them to sit. He didn't waste time once they were in place.

"Good morning," Dom said. "I know this directive was sudden. At the same time, it's vital. I'm looking forward to hearing what you guys plan to do about it."

As Rolland and Monroe had discussed, Rolland took the lead in laying out the strategy. He went into detail about the extensive monitoring of Brad—the activity and discovery targets, how the CRM system would be used to hold him accountable to the desired results. He emphasized that Brad would have both a plan and a way of knowing where he stood at all times.

Dom nodded, and Rolland pivoted to Janet.

"Monroe and I spoke at length on how we should use the CRM system to really grow Janet's capabilities going forward," he said. "She's already good at getting in the door with prospects once she puts her mind to it, so we need to make sure that she's exposing herself to enough opportunities to be able to bring about the results she wants in the end.

"Once she's in the door, it seems she builds good rapport and sometimes that's good enough for the client to buy. But other times, she hasn't really dug deep enough to truly understand the client's need, evaluate what they'd be willing to spend to solve that need, and ensure she has the right people at the buying table who are going to be involved in making such a decision."

Rolland tried to gauge how Dom was receiving the information. The boss didn't give any facial cues, so Rolland plunged onward.

"Similar to Brad, we want to make sure she's having thorough Discovery meetings. We don't really have the face-to-face issue with her; if anything, we would like to see her being more efficient with the meetings she is conducting. Therefore, we'd prefer to measure how many proposals she delivers with a sales engineer involved. Because, what we've noticed is, in order to augment Janet's bubbly sales persona—which customers like—we need to also have someone in the room with all of the technical service knowledge, which customers trust.

"If we do that," Rolland finished, "we'll be able to give her coaching tips over time based on what the data suggests. Unlike how we will present the plan to Brad, with Janet our plan is to go through a complete territory planning process that starts with her personal goals and links those goals all the way to the behaviors and activities that she needs to perform on a daily and weekly basis to be successful. We believe that if she connects the plan to her own motivations, she will see this as a positive program."

As Rolland finished, he felt flush with pride. *Great job!* he thought. *Just a month or two with Monroe and already I'm sounding like a seasoned sales executive in front of Dom.*

That made Dom's reaction all the more startling.

"Good analysis," Dom began. "But—" His face turned crimson, and a frown burrowed deep into his forehead. "But I'm not sure I got *my* point across. Maybe you can explain to me what part of that plan is going to turn around our bottom line in the next three weeks. I'm not hearing it. I told you guys I'm comfortable with the long-term plans you're working on. That's not why we're here. What I wanted to hear this morning was specifically what we're going to do to stem the bleeding."

After Dom spoke, there was a brief, respectful silence. Rolland's self-congratulations evaporated. *That stings,* he thought. *But Dom's right. If only I could've known a year ago what I know now. I could've gotten out ahead of all this so Dom wouldn't be in this position. If I can't turn this, I won't be around to see the fruits of this work with Monroe.*

Monroe calmly reached out and touched Rolland's cuff, then looked to Dom. "I believe Rolland had one other vital part to this plan that you'll be interested in, Dom. Do you want to go ahead and share that, Rolland, or should I?"

The question brought Rolland back into the moment. "No, I've got it. I was just so excited about the first piece that I lost track. I apologize." He flashed a contrite smile. "Part of getting the salespeople to document their current sales into CRM initially is also to provide me the direct input I need for choosing our best, most immediate opportunities. Then, with that information, I will cooperatively engage and sell those deals with the sales reps. I might talk to Enrique and see if he'd be willing to partner up on one or two of them, too. That will bring immediacy to the opportunities that can swiftly improve our numbers."

By Dom's exhale, Rolland knew he'd finally hit the point the boss wanted to hear. "That sounds like a really good idea, guys," Dom said. "I agree that Enrique certainly has a great amount of expertise he can pass along. It's not his typical role, but I think he'd be open to helping us in that way. I'll make sure I touch base with him so he understands what we're all trying to accomplish and why it's important for him to help us out.

"And while this is a good idea, I'd like to hear from you next week, Rolland. Once you've got these deals in place and the plan rolling, I'd like to get your opinion on how it's all going because we need to have something break through fast. Monroe, would you be available to circle back with us as well?"

"Unfortunately, Dom, I apologize, but I will be on vacation out of the country," Monroe said. "Rolland has my cell number, though, if something comes up."

"Not a problem, that sounds great," Dom said. His relief at the turn in the meeting was palpable. "I'm sure you deserve it. Enjoy your time away." Dom turned back to Rolland. "So you'll get that meeting with me set, right?"

"Absolutely."

Dom thanked them again and then released them. In the hallway, Monroe and Rolland shook hands.

"Told you," Monroe said with a big grin.

"It was a little dicey there for a minute," Rolland said, mimicking wiping down his brow. "Thanks for the prompt."

"You'd have found your way to it. I just closed up the distance a little." Monroe now took on a look of deeper gravity. "Now, remember, Rolland: as you're meeting with the team members, you'll only get out of them what they're willing to give you. We've talked about this before, right? You can never want success more for someone than they want it for themselves."

B EFORE THE PLANNING MEETINGS COMMENCED, ROLLAND TOOK A DEEP dive into each sales rep's deals, whether completed or pending. He wanted to make sure he had a firm understanding of what reasonable expectations should look like for each of them. While Rolland was holed up with background material, Sarah set up the meetings.

"I'd like to see Brad first," Rolland had told her. Brad's program was the one that required the most planning, and Rolland was curious to see how Brad would take to a system in which he and his progress were more closely monitored.

When Rolland laid everything out—the increased activity monitoring, more in-person interaction with Rolland, the CRM components—Brad surprised him with an enthusiastic reception.

"I think I can really show how we can use the CRM system to monitor funnel flow and activity," he told Rolland. "This is why I've been so gung-ho about the system these last few months."

"I appreciate that, Brad," Rolland said. "But this also means we'll be having more frequent checkups—Post-Call Debriefs, Funnel Reviews, and the like. We're adding to your plate and setting some accountability bars here. You need to know that."

"Understood," Brad said. Rolland noticed a quiver in Brad's voice; the gravity of the situation was getting through.

"I also thought it would be fun to have a rewards system in place for when you hit your marks."

"It … all sounds good to me, it really does." Brad stammered just a little as he said this. "The targets you've laid out seem attainable to me."

He seems to be convincing himself, Rolland thought, *but I wonder how* real *Brad's assessment is*. On one hand, Rolland was thrilled with the professed buy-in. On the other, he'd heard overconfidence and bravado from Brad before, with few outcomes that warranted those reactions. Now, with measurable goals and accountability tied to them, Rolland knew Brad couldn't just talk the talk.

This will be the final test, Rolland thought. *Either he steps up and meets these standards, or...*

Rolland didn't need to finish the thought.

When Rolland ushered Brad out, he found Janet sitting in a chair outside his door, waiting. He took note of her curiosity upon seeing Brad, as if she were trying to suss out what awaited her. She came into Rolland's office and sat down.

"Back-to-back meetings, Rolland?" she asked. "What's the agenda?"

Rolland appreciated the direct question; it meant he could get right to it rather than going through an unnecessary introduction.

"We've got a big challenge, Janet," he said. "We need to get our numbers up, and fast. I'm viewing this as an opportunity, for all of us. I'd like to take some time together to set up some goals and map out a sales path for achieving them."

"OK." Janet's reply struck him as tentative.

"I sense some hesitation."

"It's not that, exactly," Janet said. "Having goals and plans is always something I hear is important, but when I hear it I just think it sounds like a bunch of front-loaded work and I don't know where to start. I'm absolutely open to getting your help setting that up."

Rolland was relieved. Janet was asking for his leadership, not expressing resistance. "Excellent," he said. "And you're right about the upfront work, so this could take multiple meetings to finalize, but I'll help you through each step. Before we dive too deeply though, I want to get a feel for your current opportunities so we can identify a few to work on together."

Janet went through her existing deals, and out of those Rolland and she identified a handful that seemed particularly promising. After that, Rolland pivoted to discussing Janet's personal goals and financial aspirations, relying on Monroe's lessons about uncovering motivation.

"Right now, my biggest goal is making it to my best friend's bachelorette vacation," Janet said. "She wants the bridal party to spend a few days together in Hawaii."

"Fun!" Rolland said. "And pricey."

"The thing is," Janet said, "she's been one of my closest friends since we were kids. I really, *really* want to experience this with her. But the setup is that we all have to pay our own way and chip in to cover her costs. And that's pretty intimidating, financially speaking. At the same time, I'm thinking about maybe a getaway down the line with this guy I'm seeing. It's just a lot."

"I understand," Rolland said. "Would you say that right now, though, the bachelorette trip is the priority?"

"I would, yes."

"What kind of timetable are you looking at?" he asked.

"Nothing is set yet," Janet said. "But I figure six to nine months."

"OK," Rolland said, "that seems like enough time. Let's work backward from that goal to how your job here can affect it. How much do you think you'll need beforehand to make Hawaii possible?"

"I figured four thousand extra dollars would make it doable."

Rolland jotted the figure down. "Based on your current sales compensation, we need to determine how much extra revenue you'll need to generate to hit that mark," he said. "If you don't make this extra money, what happens?"

"If I can't comfortably commit when the maid of honor needs to start booking hotels and events, I'll either have to ask them to push back the trip—which would be a nightmare, given the time-table—or I'll just have to send my regrets. I don't even want to con-template disappointing my friend like that."

"Let's focus on making it happen, then," Rolland said, offering her a warm smile. "Now that we know what you need in additional sales requirement, let's map out together all of the selling steps nec-essary for you to achieve the increase. Based on your typical sales success, how many quotes and presentations will it take for you to close that level of sales? And from there, how many Discovery meetings and new prospects will it take to generate those quotes? Does that make sense?"

"Yes, I follow." Janet worked out the math and determined what it would take for her to reach her goals. Rolland wrote down the metrics.

"Great," he said. "Let's distribute those numbers into monthly and quarterly targets for you so you can keep track of your prog-ress. I'll gladly partner with you to help you stay on course and successfully meet your goal. My wife and I have been to Hawaii for an anniversary vacation, and I can't imagine a better place for you and your friends to go. I'm *so* excited for you. Let's make it a reality."

Janet's face lit up at Rolland's enthusiasm for her goals. "Sounds great. Thanks, Rolland," she said. "I really appreciate it."

"I'm happy we can work on this together," Rolland said. "Hey, another thing while I'm thinking about it: I notice that most mornings you come in with coffee. How about we put some Starbucks gift cards on the line as you hit initial successes with these short-term goals?"

Janet let out an entertained snicker. "Works for me. I never turn down a free coffee, so I'll be going for it!"

As they put Janet's plan down in detail, Rolland showed her how he'd identified Discovery meetings and leveraging sales engineers as areas that could help boost her success. She openly agreed to use those metrics for her part in the challenge. The buy-in to his vision from Brad and Janet left Rolland feeling invigorated. Now, he just needed them to demonstrate their own true desire to see the accomplishments become reality.

Next up was Diane. He repeated most of the process with her since they'd already scheduled another onboarding meeting for that day. In short order, she and Rolland developed an initial ninety-day territory plan, and they also identified fully documented, BANTC Discovery meetings as one of her activity targets. That meeting out of the way, Rolland said to himself, "Three down, one to go tomorrow" as he headed down the hallway to look for Enrique. He wanted to share the successes with his most experienced rep before their meeting the next day.

Rolland found Enrique in the copier room.

"Got a minute?" he asked.

"Sure thing. Fire away, Rolland."

"I know we've got a meeting scheduled for tomorrow, but I'm kind of excited about the strides we've made today, so I just wanted to share."

"I'm eager to hear about it," Enrique said.

"The short story," Rolland went on, "is we're going to hold a little inner-office challenge. I've already met with the others, and we've laid out specific activity targets for them to hit over the next ninety days, along with some shorter-term goals to generate more sales in the next few weeks."

"Smart," Enrique said. "That should keep them focused."

"I think so." Rolland could feel the excitement welling up in him again. "This is the path to getting our entire team working together and taking our sales to the next level." Rolland paused, letting Enrique consider that before he continued. "Anyway, we're going to be using the CRM system to track all the activities performed for this challenge. Just for some added incentive, I've got some Starbucks gift cards that I'm going to be giving out along the way to the best performers. Tomorrow, you and I should look at your deals and pick out some things you could do to have even more success. All of us will be working together as a team toward this contest. I think this will be our approach going forward."

Enrique kept a tight smile. "It sounds like you have an interesting plan," he said. "Listen, I've got to get back at it. We'll talk tomorrow."

THAT EVENING, ENRIQUE SAT AT HOME, WATCHING HIS FAVORITE PROGRAM on TV and absorbing none of it. His mind remained fixed on what he'd heard from Rolland. He found it irritating. Worse, he wasn't sure he could sit at a meeting the next day and hear it again without blowing his top. He fished his phone out of his pocket and called Dom. His nephew had scarcely said hello before Enrique blew up.

"Your right-hand man is out there going on about keeping closer tabs on our activities and how we have to answer to that appalling machine," he said. "I've been quiet while you've all been fiddling around with your shiny CRM system. I don't need Big Brother watching my every move—that's not how family operates! If you've got a problem with the way I'm selling, you can come talk to me. You don't need to send Rolland down to bribe me with Starbucks cards! I don't need any fancy coffee. That's ridiculous. Are you trying to force me toward retirement faster?"

"Whoa, whoa, hang on. Activity targets? Starbucks cards?"

"That's what he's talking about," Enrique fumed.

"Just give me a second here," Dom said. Enrique said nothing, just pinching his face into a frown while he waited for Dom to open things up again.

"Uncle Enrique," Dom said at last, "has our family ever held back from talking straight with each other?"

"Not until now, no."

"Well," Dom said, exhaling "rest assured, I did not send Rolland in to do this. I didn't know he was going to pull you into the contest. That's to benefit the other sales team members, and your role was simply to assist them in closing deals. I'll talk to Rolland and get this figured out."

"I hope you do, fast. This isn't going to fly for me."

"I understand," Dom said. "But, listen, you may have overheard Carlos and I talking about how our numbers have been down in sales. I'll sort this out with Rolland. But whatever you can do to help him and get the rest of the team doing their part, I'd really appreciate you giving it some due consideration."

Enrique's breathing settled down a bit. "Are we in trouble?" he asked.

"Nothing we can't climb out of. Rolland's working hard to get it turned around. He needs your help."

Enrique chewed on his lip. He'd given his nephews their big break, then come aboard at Arachnid and was writing a wonderful closing chapter to his career. His sense of outrage yielded to a sense of duty.

"I'll do whatever I can to help," he said. "Thanks for hearing me out, Dom."

ROLLAND ARRIVED AT ARACHNID THE NEXT MORNING FULL OF TREPIDA- tion, so much so that he only nodded at Sarah's customary morning greeting. He'd received a text from Dom the night before: *Don't talk to Enrique tomorrow until you've met with me.* He'd replied *OK*, and then spent the entire night trying to find consistent sleep.

Dom asked Rolland into his office and relayed the conversation with Enrique from the night before. Rolland's heart sank.

"I supported you and tried to pull back the reins on Enrique," Dom said. "I trust you to figure this out and get him back on board. He was hopping mad, and I do understand why. I didn't know you'd be including him on an activity-based contest. You and I both know how he feels about the CRM. Coffee just isn't going to bring him around."

"I'm sorry," Rolland said. "I was just so excited about the buy-in from others that I think I misspoke."

"It went over like a nuclear bomb," Dom said. "You and Enrique need to work together to get us out of this slump. I don't have time for you to not be on the same page. Get it handled."

Rolland left Dom's office dismayed and discouraged. He'd set out to motivate the team and establish well-founded plans for each sales rep to attack. And now it could all be undone because he'd inadvertently angered his best salesman.

Rolland didn't want to have to do it, but he saw few good options and not much time left.

He picked up his phone and dialed.

O N A BEACH CHAIR IN COSTA DEL SOL, WITH A COCKTAIL IN THE CUPHOLD-er and his left hand holding that of his wife in the adjacent chair, Monroe settled in and gazed across the water. Europe had always been a far-off dream for them, the stuff of fanciful notions and one-day-we'll-get-there chats. And now…

His phone buzzed in his shirt pocket.

"I'm not answering," he said.

The phone buzzed again.

"At least see who it is," his wife said.

Monroe frowned, then reached in his pocket and retrieved the phone. He took note of the caller ID.

"This better be good," he said. He pressed the button on the screen.

Takeaways

The Boss Lays It on the Line

Accountability
Partnership and Planning

NO MATTER HOW STRONG AND WELL-INTENDED YOUR PLANS FOR THE FU-ture, present-day concerns can be hard to see beyond. Dom is a forward-looking, generally hands-off boss. He believes in what Monroe and Rolland are doing. However, he has pressing sales concerns that need fast answers. To that end, Dom suggests using CRM to hold people accountable.

> Accountability Partnerships help people hold themselves accountable to their own goals and produce results through the partnership.

Recall that Accountability is one of the two walls in the Team Balloon Model that can be used to lift the balloons higher when proper pressure is applied. I say "proper pressure" because most of the time, when thinking about accountability, people imagine holding someone's feet to the fire. In that scenario it's one person with power over another, holding them in a position that is definitely undesirable. I call that Impositional Accountability.

The alternative: an Accountability Partnership, which is about helping people hold themselves accountable to their own goals and producing results through the partnership. We'll also talk about the four keys of effective accountability, how to have the most effective Discovery meetings using BANTC, the importance of good planning meetings, and how to use gamification effectively.

For accountability to be a true partnership it needs to be positioned appropriately. Rolland wasn't prepared to do this right. He had the wrong mindset, thinking of accountability as something to be imposed. In his words, "When you start measuring how many face-to-face meetings a salesperson has, that seems like a remedial plan." But an Accountability Partnership is a team effort based on mutual interest, working with your salespeople to define and pursue their dreams.

It's easy to throw around the concept of "goals." However, as we discussed in our Takeaways chapter with Allison, a genuine future goal has to be something that the salesperson is emotionally connected to.

Most goals can be translated into a monetary target—how much additional income do they need to meet it? For example, if their goal is to take a month-long vacation to Europe, and they have paid vacation time for two weeks, they'll need to earn the equivalent of two weeks' unpaid time, as well as the commissions they will not make over the month. Plus, they'll have travel expenses. These figures can be calculated. From them, you can create a sales plan that will generate enough compensation for your salesperson to reach those targets.

From there on, the Accountability Partnership is redefined as what it'll take to get them to Europe for a month, not what it's going to take to meet sales goals.

The Four Keys of an Accountability Partnership

THINK OF AN ACCOUNTABILITY PARTNERSHIP AS THE HIGHEST LEVEL OF partnership you can attain with your team members. To do that, there are four sequential keys that must be attained. We refer to these as keys because until the employee is with you and agrees to move to the next level, you cannot unlock that level of partnership. Without these keys, you may have to go back to Impositional Accountability.

The Four Keys are:

» **Standards are Understood**, meaning that both you and your team member know what is expected at all times.
» **Regular Review**, in which you agree upon a time to evaluate what has been done, or not done.
» **Rewards**: the positive outcome, treat or privilege will be the result of meeting the standards.
» **Consequences**: the negative outcome that will result in the standards not being met.

The first key is a positive interaction: the partner sets their own goals and understands that it's for their benefit. The second key tilts toward the negative. The third key is another positive reinforcement. You don't want to follow a review, which can be negative, with a punishment. That would be two negative interactions in a row. Therefore, the next step is to offer a positive incentive.

If adding rewards still doesn't get the job done, there is a Fourth Key: consequences. With any accountability program consequences can exist, but the difference with a partnership is that the partner must be involved in defining those consequences. There's no sense implementing a consequence if your partner won't respond to it. So, rather than imposing punishment, have a conversation.

Here's an example of the Four Keys in action:

If a husband sets a goal to go to the gym twice a week, but then the weekend comes and he's comfortably reclined watching football after going only once, there are a couple of ways his wife can respond. As a partner, her first step should be to remind him of his goals and see if that is enough to refocus his behavior.

Key One to unlocking influence is to make sure the standards are understood for attaining their goals. Did the husband say he was going to go to the gym twice a week? How is he defining the "week"? Do they both have a clear understanding of how much weight he wants to lose? She isn't looking to hold him accountable; *she's looking to help him hold himself accountable*. If the reminder isn't sufficiently influencing his behavior, then she can ask if he's open to unlocking **Key Two**—regular review.

She could suggest, "Would it help if on Friday nights before the week is over, we followed up with each other how many times you've been to the gym? That way you're clearly aware of where you stand with your goals before it's too late to do something about it." If **Key Two** doesn't achieve the desired outcomes, then you move onto the next level of your partnership.

While **Key Three**, rewards, is a positive function, it still requires agreement from the partner. Keep in mind that if Key Two is sufficient to make sure standards are being met, then there's no reason to go to the next key because adding a reward seems like an unnecessary bribe. On the other hand, if the Friday-night follow-up *isn't* working, then offering a reward such as watching a favorite movie for future success could be the answer.

Sometimes, even a reward isn't enough to achieve the outcomes you and your partner want, and it's necessary to move onto **Key Four**—consequences. In our scenario, the wife should ask, "The reward I offered was unsuccessful. Do you want to meet this goal strongly enough that it'd make sense to put some sort of consequence to you if you miss the mark next time?" Letting him self-impose the consequence allows him to remain in the driver's seat toward his own goals.

Consequences can escalate if they must, but the partner should always have been involved, and not be surprised by any consequences that occur.

To recap, let's look at how this process specifically pertains to salespeople:

>> **Key One – Make Sure the Standards Are Understood:** Your salesperson has to be involved in this process. Once they've bought in, there needs to be an accessible scoreboard, or tracking mechanism, so you and they will always know where they stand.

>> **Key Two – Regular Review:** Scoreboards are useful only if they're checked. You need to have regular, consistent reviews to measure progress relative to standards. Otherwise, you can't make periodic adjustments to the strategy to keep on track with achieving goals.

>> **Key Three – Rewards:** Rewarding positive behavior can increase the salesperson's commitment to the next level. Beyond compensation, rewards can exist in the form of praise, public recognition, being taken out for lunch, etc. Not everyone is motivated solely by money!

>> **Key Four – Consequences:** You have to accept that at some

point consequences will need to be a part of the program. At the same time, you should never jump straight to Key Four from Key One.

These keys are an escalation in accountability. What you should find is that the more experienced salespeople who want to succeed and are self-motivated don't require going much further than making sure both parties agree on the standards. That might be enough for them to hold themselves accountable.

If your accountability partnership seems to be progressing through the keys, make sure that you've tried to effectively implement each one before jumping to the next. In some instances, if you reach Key Four especially with top salespeople, you'll find that either their goal wasn't actually very compelling (so no level of accountability would get them to strive for it) or there is something else holding them back. Watch for signs of either so that you can update their sales plan or help them in your mentoring sessions to overcome whatever's impeding their success.

So far in our story, Rolland is focused on tackling Key One with his team. Since Brad is in the Assess Balloon, Rolland essentially defined the standards for him as expectations. With Janet, he invested more time in working with her to come up with standards that would improve her sales success and steer her toward a personal goal. Not all reps should be held to the same standards, but how should you go about defining them? The best practice for Key One is to hold each of your salespeople to one of the three categories in the Standards Scale:

» **Results:** Where they are being evaluated on the outcomes they produce.
» **Key Funnel Metrics:** Where they are being evaluated on the different steps in their funnel.
» **Activities:** Where they are being evaluated on how they spend their time.

What you choose to measure for each salesperson will depend on their experience and their degree of personal accountability. With your Service Balloon salespeople, since you're giving them the greatest authority and responsibility, you typically hold them accountable for results. If Rolland wanted to bring Enrique in as part of the accountability program he was establishing, it would've been best to simply measure Enrique's results rather than getting himself into trouble by incorrectly suggesting activities. Because that wasn't the case, Enrique felt disrespected and the accountability program lacked a sense of partnership.

> Choose what to measure for each salesperson based on their experience and personal accountability.

If a salesperson isn't responding to being accountable for their results alone, the next step is to manage and measure their key funnel metrics. This middle tier of measurement refers to close ratios, forecast accuracy, and funnel size and shape. This is the approach that Rolland took with Janet. She helped determine the metrics that she was comfortable striving for. The goal is to see periodic improvement in the categories being measured.

Improving a salesperson's efficiency will reduce the time and effort required to make each sale. If sufficient improvement is demonstrated within a reasonable length of time, then the metrics can be adjusted to address other areas, or the salesperson could even move up to being measured for their results.

Brad was the initial subject for the accountability partnership. Brad's lack of production and placement in the Assess Balloon dictates that he should be monitored at the lowest level, i.e. activities. When you are monitoring activities, you may be setting the standards that need to be met. Rolland does this for Brad because Brad needs to demonstrate that he's motivated to get back into the Partner Balloon.

Partner and Service Balloon salespeople don't need minimum requirements to be set because they've already proven they are above those bars. So, they should be given the flexibility to set their own targets and strive for their own goals. When Rolland requires Brad to hold a set number of face-to-face meetings and to document each of his Discovery meetings, he is doing so to make sure Brad is fulfilling the minimum best practices for closing sales. If you are in the same position as Rolland, you need to figure out what aspects of the sales process your rep is struggling with and what the best-practice activities would help them close sales. What tasks should a salesperson perform in each stage to positively interact with their customers?

At any point in the Accountability Partnership, you can adjust the level of the standards being monitored or even which Key is being implemented. Is your salesperson is reaching their end goal? If you ever find yourself moving down the standards scale toward funnel metrics or activities, remember that your salesperson's new goal is to meet these numbers, not necessarily make those numbers result in more sales. This can be a struggle for sales managers because their mind is always on the end game. However, if you set a target to make twenty cold calls and the salesperson completes the task in time, then they have accomplished your targets no matter what sales come as a result. Then you may need to alter the activities targets to better attain the results you want.

BANTC

BRAD AND JANET WILL BE MONITORED FOR HAVING THOROUGH DISCOVERY Meetings. That may seem like a broad metric, meaning that it's difficult to document and measure. However, the ISM system identifies a specific way to measure the attainment of influential discovery through the sales process. By influential discovery, I mean that we distinguish between what's *believed* vs. what is *known*. Before a sale is qualified to exit the Discovery Stage, you need to know as much as possible about BANTC.

> » **Budget** – how willing a prospect is to take tradeoffs to accomplish their goals.
> » **Authority** – how sure are we that we have strong advocacy from all relevant parties to purchase from us.
> » **Needs** – what emotional level the prospect feels about their needs that we can uniquely address.
> » **Timeframe** – what costs and problems will occur if the prospect waits longer to make a decision.
> » **Credibility** – why and how strongly does the customer feel about including you in the buying process.

AND FOR ALL OF THIS, YOU NEED TO GATHER ACTUAL EVIDENCE—NOT JUST hopes, guesses and assumptions!

Rolland alluded to these factors when he told Dom that Janet "hasn't really dug deep enough to truly understand the client's need, evaluate what they'd be willing to spend to solve that need, and ensure she has the right people at the buying table who are going to be involved in making such a decision." The second component is how influential that information is likely to be toward securing the sale. Sales are lost because the measurement of one of these factors was either not as strong as it was thought to be—or not as strong as a competitor was able to attain.

Authority and **Needs** are the first two factors to address when it comes to gaining insight, and you address them simultaneously. You want to talk to many people in the organization to gain a 360-degree perspective of a company's need. When you're ready to dig deeper, though, make sure that the proper decision-making authority is part of the conversation. They have to understand the pain of the need in their own mind in order to be willing to spend resources on the solution you are selling. In other words, it needs to be bothering them, and you need to be able to show them how that pain or annoyance can stop.

> People buy on emotions and justify with logic.

Once you've identified the authority, your goal is to get them to share what needs they emotionally connect to. People buy on emotions and justify with logic. Everyone from the bottom of the ladder up will have an opinion about the company's needs that you'll want to understand to provide the best solution. But only the authority can sign off on a deal, so adjust your priorities accordingly.

Budget and **Timeframe** are two factors that heavily depend on the authority's perception of the importance and urgency of the problem you propose to solve for them. This is why they are generally collected after you have a strong attainment of Authority and Needs. The greater the emotional impact the need has on the authority, the greater the budget is likely to be for addressing that need. Budget goes beyond money. The authority could be giving up time, resources that would otherwise go toward other projects, or even prior relationships with other vendors. Further, there will be more urgency to solve the need if the authority faces a deadline. Some sort of government-imposed deadline is much more pressing than an unpublished goal for the implementation of a solution. Urgency and tradeoffs for your solution are important to understand.

Credibility requires constant attention and improvement

throughout the sales process. You begin establishing it the moment you approach your first contact at a company. Every individual you address has the potential to throw support toward your offering. At the same time, if anyone feels you haven't built credibility with them, they can protest what you're bringing to the table. For each opportunity your salespeople pursue, you should get them to think about and document where they believe they are in terms of evidence and score for each of these five factors.

Whatever the standards that you choose to set and are agreed upon with each salesperson, they need to be well-documented. I mentioned earlier that a scoreboard, or something like it, was necessary in order to regularly review progress, but that's not the only benefit to documenting! If you and your accountability partner are not clearly on the same page regarding standards, it *will* create problems later on. Writing them down makes the standards indisputable so that the strategy does not unintentionally shift over time.

Lastly, as many studies have shown, having your salesperson write down those goals—and share them with you—will make them "incredibly more likely to follow through." That's what Monroe told Rolland in regard to Janet.

Sales Focus Blueprints

NSTITUTING AN ACCOUNTABILITY PARTNERSHIP IS FOUNDED ON BUILDING Sales Focus Blueprints (SFB) with each of your sales reps. In the absence of an SFB, the standards that you set are merely nice ideas. With the many distractions a salesperson faces each day, the only way for them to hold fast to their targets is to have an intentional plan they can refer to. Monroe raised a fair question: "Janet shows promise, but do you believe she comes into work each day with a set game plan?" Real, integrated planning can take several one-on-one meetings to nail down the first time around, but it's one of the best ways to create a predictive model of sales results that can then be monitored. Thus, each year ISM recommends conducting a Sales Focus Blueprint Meeting with each of your salespeople. This meeting may take place over several get-togethers, but generally proceeds through three phases.

The **first phase** of Sales Focus Blueprint meetings is to demonstrate the significance of having a blueprint to your salesperson. Too many salespeople run around *reacting* to their marketplace, so one of the greatest improvements they could make for increasing their sales success would be getting organized and intentional (in other words, *proactive*) with their daily activities. Salespeople must move beyond "tyranny of the urgent" and prioritize their time around their goals. Failing to do this makes them reactive and the outcome at the end of the day will have little to do with what they hoped for and everything to do with what fell in their lap.

The **second phase** of the SFB meetings is establishing the salesperson's real personal goals. What is the "Why" behind their plan? *You can't want something for someone more than they want it for themselves.* For Janet, her "Why" was a vacation in Hawaii. Through your mentoring and coaching sessions, you should already have a strong sense of what drives your salespeople. If not, this phase of the meeting can be a great start to your mentoring relationship.

> The goals you set for a salesperson will never override the ones they have set for themselves.

The key here is to ensure that they are not reciting your goals or the company's goals. The goals must be felt personally, or the salesperson won't feel as obliged to hold themselves to them. From there, emphasize that you're in this *together* to achieve their goals because their plan is also becoming your plan. Janet's plan for selling enough to afford a bachelorette getaway directly contributes to Rolland's annual forecast and the company's overarching goals. Don't think for a moment that the goals you have for your salesperson are going to override the goals they have for themselves. If their goals are higher than your quota, then that's what you're working toward with them. If their goals are lower than your quota, it's *still* what you're working toward, but you should probably consider what other team planning you'll need to do to make up the difference.

Phase three is to back into goals using the compensation plan. Referring to Janet, Monroe said, "You need to identify her long-term goals and help her connect the dots from those goals to the sales actions necessary to reach them." Many capable salespeople know what's required to sell and they can also tell you exactly what they desire. At the same time, most never take the time to map out an estimated number of *activities* to go through the stages from calling on prospects to hitting their desired sales figures.

This conversation requires mediation from the manager, especially when working with younger salespeople. Your salespeople should know what industries your company specializes in and what revenue streams are available to them. So, help them plan out which segments optimize their time and maximize their commissions. If you work backwards from the total amount of commissions they want to earn and the respective number of sales to hit that target, then you can divide that amongst the various revenue streams the salesperson can use. From there, you can work backwards with each revenue stream to identify the numbers they need to achieve at each stage of the sales process. This is where assumptions come in because, for example, you and your salesperson have to decide how many delivered proposals will convert into a customer actually buying.

To further that example: If you need to deliver four proposals to make a sale, how many Collaboration meetings need to be held to advance four deals to the proposal stage? The best estimates in terms of conversions and closing ratios come from having field experience. Salespeople are naturally optimistic so their expectations, if unchecked, could be unrealistic and kill their motivation. Also, make sure that all numbers in the plan are believed by the salesperson. Otherwise, it's going to be *your* plan for *how* to get them results.

After you've worked through creating long-term plans with each member of your team, **Phase four** of Sales Focus Blueprint Meetings is to create an activity calendar for those who will be held accountable at the activity standard. Depending on which balloon your salesperson is in, you may work all the way back up the process with them to defining the number of calls they'll need to make. Balance how granular the plan gets with the level of accountability standards being applied.

Some top-performing salespeople may be open to creating a full-fledged blueprint if they're interested in further developing certain aspects of their process, but not all will be. When you measure a salesperson at the activity level, these calendars will establish checkpoints to help them stay on track. You always want your plans to provide your salesperson with advanced warning if they're getting out of alignment with the standards they need to meet. That way they can take corrective action instead of being blindsided by consequences.

An activity calendar can be month-to-month or quarter-to-quarter. Remember, Key Two for an effective Accountability Partnership is **Regular Review**. Activity Review meetings and Funnel Review meetings can regularly check whether reality aligns with expectations. (We'll go deeper into those in the Epilogue.) If an original plan no longer makes sense, adjustments may need to be made to certain ratios to get the salesperson back on track. A best practice is for the salesperson to create the activity calendar on their own and bring it back to you—again, making your team involved in their own accountability. Some salespeople will front-load their calendar while others will put off starting the activities until later in the year. Either way, challenge their plan and see what their backup is in case they fall short. A template that can be useful in guiding you through the steps of an SFB is available at this book's Companion Resource website—www.acultureofpredictablesales.com.

At the start of this chapter we revisited the concept of the Team Balloon Model. Accountability needs to be applied equally with Support for the model to work. In some instances, setting standards and demonstrating how those standards will contribute to a salesperson's eventual success is sufficient for motivating them. Janet even acknowledged the importance of goals and plans in taking her where she wanted to go; she just didn't know where to start. At some level, even Brad is aware of his shortcomings, and that setting targets and plans will benefit his sales.

Rewards (Key Three) can enhance the success of an Accountability Partnership. Rolland brought up the idea of rewarding Brad for successes and Monroe agreed. Rolland decided he would make an inter-office challenge out of it to further stimulate his team's efforts. However, remember that rewards should only be used *when they will be well-received* by each salesperson.

Gamification

REWARDS AND THE GAMES, SALES CONTESTS, AND PROMOTIONS THAT ARE established for earning them, can be seen as cheesy stunts. Many managers perceive that games are just for less-experienced or less-proficient salespeople, which would have perhaps meant

Rolland was right in incorporating them into his plans for Brad and Janet. He was looking to balance the long-term rewards of success with a small dose of instant gratification. Gamification itself is not unprofessional; what matters is how it is interpreted and executed. So, start by modeling a positive attitude yourself, but don't overdo it. Let's break down Rolland's challenge to see what he did right and where he went wrong.

ISM uses the concept of a Rewards Diamond. Like in a baseball diamond, you have to round all four bases to be credited with hitting a home run. That's the best result, to round all of the bases to score a run in one go, but any hit that gets you on base is an excellent start. When it comes to designing a professional sales contest, setting a foundation of rules is like getting on **first base**. It's a minimum requirement to avoid an out. You can't play a game if you don't understand the parameters—how to win, how much time you have, what isn't fair play, etc. Rolland was on the right track with setting the foundation for his challenge. He had defined activity targets for his reps and he placed a time limit on reaching those targets.

Rolland could have just introduced his challenge to Brad and he would have been fine. He wanted to go further, though, and raise the stakes by involving more participants. He told Monroe, "Salespeople are competitive; they won't want to let any of the others beat them." At some level, everyone is naturally competitive.

By bringing competition into his challenge, Rolland reached **second base** in his design. It will greatly increase the passion and investment your sales team brings to the table. However, it's critical that the basis of the competition feels *relevant*. If you're an Olympic swimmer and someone challenges you to swim across a resort pool, it won't seem like much of a competition. Rolland ran afoul of Enrique when he suggested Enrique would be participating in the competition based on hitting activity targets the same way Brad would. To a top seller like Enrique, such activities feel beneath them.

Reaching **third base** means you need to create value for your salespeople that they wouldn't be able to get otherwise. When you create value, you motivate your team to divert from their normal course to focus on your target. Sometimes value is substantially present in the salesperson's own goal-setting. They see what they want and are willing to make. Value can also be created in the form of a reward, but only if it has perceived significance to the people aiming for it.

With his challenge, Rolland tripped on his way to third base. Bard and Janet recognized that making changes to the way they sold would generate more success and income for them. And there isn't anything wrong with gift cards. Rolland intended for the cards to be tokens of the recognition that Brad and Janet desired. He did not perceive that any of his salespeople would work toward their goals solely because they coveted $25 worth of coffee.

> Rewards that offer little challenge or whose value is not representative of the cost appear to salespeople as gimmicks.

The value of a reward has to exceed the cost of the salesperson's effort and the effort required cannot be equal to the salesperson's regular routine. Otherwise, *there isn't any challenge to overcome* and the reward appears to be a gimmick. This is the other half of the reason Rolland lost Enrique. First, he suggested to Enrique that they would decide which of his activities to track via CRM—but Enrique is a top performer in the Service Balloon and should be held accountable for his results, not his activities. Then, to make matters worse, Enrique was offended that Rolland came "to bribe me with Starbucks cards! I don't need any fancy coffee." Since he didn't perceive any sales-development benefits in being tracked on his activities nor any benefit in receiving recognition for winning an easy competition, Rolland's offer had the opposite effect—Enrique felt underappreciated and insulted.

Enrique's involvement in Rolland's challenge should have been as a mentor and partner to the younger salespeople. That was Dom's perception as well. He told Rolland that "Enrique certainly has a great amount of expertise he can pass along. It's not his typical role, but I think he'd be open to helping us in that way." He also went on to say that Rolland should frame Enrique's role in a way that communicated the value of his participation. Had Rolland successfully conveyed that to Enrique instead of doing what he did, he would have been *so* close to reaching home plate with his challenge. **Home plate** in a game's design is to instill a sense of camaraderie.

Whether people are working together during the challenge

or simply reaping the rewards as a group, there is a shared interest. Camaraderie adds a social aspect to your sales contest. It grows stronger bonds and it establishes deeper lines of accountability for succeeding in the contest. Of course, not all contests have to be home runs; getting on base is better than not hitting at all. Analyzing and creating your games and sales contests by using the Rewards Diamond can help you avoid a number of pitfalls and allow you to properly use rewards within your team.

Let's return to the final Key in your Accountability Partnerships. Clear standards, Sales Focus Blueprints, games and the rest don't always get the improved outcomes you want, and you need to go to the Fourth Key: Consequences. Now, not all consequences are extreme. Just as value in a game must match the effort people will be putting in, so consequences have to match the shortfall. As you implement Key Four with someone, slowly increase the level of consequence to keep pace with the level of shortfall. If you fail to do so, then in effect you're allowing the salesperson to fail until the shortfall is so dramatic that only one last consequence is appropriate. Sudden termination will come as a shock to them, and it shouldn't.

Sometimes, parts of an intended reward can have the effect of consequences at a lower level. For example, if all Arachnid salespeople had to enter their progress into a CRM system that was visible to everyone, then everyone would know if anyone were slacking off. This is a subtle technique, but it can modify behavior. Other forms of consequences could be self-imposed by the salesperson or, as discussed earlier, scaling back a salesperson's joint-accountability standards from results back to key metrics or even specific activity requirements.

Imposing unilateral consequences reduces your ability to coach and mentor effectively.

In extreme situations, formal final warnings are necessary. And if the behavior persists, termination is the final option. That can be a hard pill to swallow, as witnessed by Rolland's reluctance to go there with Brad. Be careful: If the consequence isn't mutually agreed on as appropriate, they can reduce your ability to coach and mentor. Unless Key One has been employed, and the standards are understood and agreed upon, consequences erode trust.

Overview of the Concepts in This Chapter

» **Accountability Partnership**

- Positioning: mindset and terminology
- Four Keys
    - **Standards are Understood** – meaning that both you and your team member know what is expected at all times
        - Standards Scale
            - Results
            - Key Funnel Metrics
            - Activities
    - **Regular Review** – where you agree upon a time to evaluate what has been done, or not done
    - **Rewards** – the positive outcome, treat or privilege will be the result of meeting the standards
    - **Consequences** – the negative outcome that will result in the standards not being met

» **Discovery Meetings**

- BANTC with supporting evidence
    - **Budget** – how willing a prospect is to take tradeoffs to accomplish their goals.
    - **Authority** – how sure are we that we have strong advocacy from all relevant parties to purchase from us
    - **Needs** – what emotional level does the prospect feel about their needs that we can uniquely address
    - **Timeframe** – what costs and problems will occur if the prospect waits longer to make a decision
    - **Credibility** – why and how strongly does the customer feel about including you in the buying process

» **Sales Focus Blueprint Meetings Phases**

- Building the territory plan
- Establishing buy-in
- Backing into goals
- Creating an Activity Calendar

» **Gamification**

- Gamesmanship is not unprofessional as long as it's not trinkety
- Designing a Sales Contest: The Rewards Diamond
    - **First Base:** The Foundation
    - **Second Base:** Competition
    - **Third Base:** Create Value
    - **Fourth Base:** Camaraderie

CHAPTER FIVE

An Old Salesman's New Tricks

"**H**ELLO, ROLLAND." MONROE TRIED TO KEEP THE WORDS CORDIAL even though he was surprised that an interruption to his vacation had come so quickly.

"Hi, Monroe. Um, I'm really sorry to bother you. How are things going?"

"Better than for you, I'm guessing," Monroe said. "I'm on the Mediterranean coast. It feels like paradise. What can I do for you?"

Rolland cleared his throat. "I promise, I wouldn't have called if it weren't important." Now the words came fast and frustrated. "I spoke with everyone on the team about the activity challenge, the way you and I planned, and somehow I set off Enrique. He went to Dom, and now I'm on his bad side, too. I feel like I took one step forward and two steps back."

Monroe made a quick decision to set aside any snark. He had a worried manager on the line, and that wasn't going to be good for anyone. "Let's slow down with the self-recrimination," he said. His wife leaned in and met eyes with him, concerned. He smiled, trying to reassure her. "What I'm hearing is Dom and Enrique aren't happy. That's not good, so let's figure out what went wrong and how we fix it. What was your approach with Enrique?"

Monroe's hope that his calm approach would transfer to Rolland appeared to bear a bit of fruit. The Arachnid sales manager slowed down and told the story.

"I met up with him in the copier room," he said. "We weren't scheduled to meet until the next day, but man, my meetings with

Brad, Janet and Diane had gone so well that I wanted to keep the momentum up."

"OK, good," Monroe said. "I'm glad to hear about the successes with the younger reps. What happened next?"

"Well," Rolland said, "I summarized how we were all participating in an activity-based inner-office challenge to take sales to the next level. I said I'd be looking to Enrique to participate in the activity and that we'd discuss it further the next morning."

"How did you describe Enrique's involvement?"

"My thinking was it'd be simple and straightforward," Rolland said, getting agitated again. "But apparently he went off and lit Dom up like a ton of dynamite and—"

Monroe cut him off. "Tell me exactly what Dom said about Enrique being upset."

"He didn't really go too deeply into it," Rolland said. "He said he'd calmed Enrique down and asked him to be more of a mentor and a peer leader to the team."

Monroe sneaked a sip of his cocktail before speaking again. "Right there, there you go, Rolland. It's not all bad. Sure, a misunderstanding occurred. But it sounds like fortunately Dom clarified the situation for him. It doesn't sound like you're really in trouble. It sounds like you just have to figure out what to do next and how to avoid repeating the mistake."

"Yeah, but—"

"The original plan was to have Enrique simply come alongside and help mentor the rest of the team," Monroe finished. "Sounds like he now knows that. But do you see how he didn't get that impression from you as you mentioned the activity aspect?"

"Sure, I get that," Rolland said, a little defensively to Monroe's ears. "But we hadn't even gotten to that yet. And wasn't Enrique supposed to be in the team contest, too? Anyway, I intended to elaborate at our scheduled meeting, which I'm having soon, which is why I wanted to talk to you first."

"I appreciate the call," Monroe said. "Unfortunately, because you didn't get to explain to him about the leadership role, he obviously saw it like this: that you'd be tracking him on specific sales activities just like the newbies. That's going to sound like something beneath a Service Balloon salesperson with as much experience and success as Enrique."

"I guess I just didn't expect such an extreme reaction since everybody else had been so positive." Rolland still sounded wounded by the episode. "Especially since I told him we'd talk more today, for goodness sakes."

Monroe softened his tone a bit. He needed to pull Rolland back into the game. "I understand where you're coming from and why you're frustrated. At the same time, I think you can get turned around on this by putting yourself in Enrique's shoes and understanding why he took it the way he did."

"I see it," Rolland conceded. "What do you think I need to do to fix it?"

"The goal is the same as it ever was: more short-term selling, while still building a long-term foundation," Monroe said. "While I think Enrique's involvement should definitely not include tracking his activities the way we would with Janet and Brad, do you think there are some some increased immediate sales-results goals we could look at with him? Those results could be tracked."

"There are probably some things he could do," Rolland agreed. "I wonder what he would think of any suggestions at this point, though."

"A fair concern," Monroe said. "The first step is clearing the air of the current issue. Why not start by apologizing for the miscommunication and clarifying your intent that he serve as a leader and a mentor? Once that's resolved, then you can do some coaching with him and see if he'd be willing to make a few small changes."

"Makes sense."

"After all," Monroe continued, "it sounds like you did really well coaching the others. Let's talk just a little bit about the difference when it comes to coaching Enrique. Coaching, just like how accountability partnerships work, differs from one salesperson to the next. There's a coaching spectrum that might help in understanding. It ranges from lecturing on the far left end, like classroom style, to merely debriefing on the far right end."

"Interesting," Rolland said.

Monroe went on. "In lecturing, you are in control of the agenda and you dictate training and action items before the salesperson moves forward. On the other side, debriefing comes after actions have been taken, plus it's driven completely by the agenda of the salesperson. Your role in that instance is to respond to their agenda and only submit questions to help them connect the dots between their identified needs and their potential solutions.

"You can see how with the other members of the team, you took greater control over the target needs and how they should go about solving them. When working with newer or weaker sales-people, we begin on the left end of the spectrum and decide to move to the right as the coaching matures. But since Enrique is in the Service Balloon, we need to handle him closer to the debriefing end of the spectrum. Only as he responds well and invites you to interact more freely with his plans should you move left on the spectrum. You don't want to pry beyond the point that he's willing to cooperate. Make sense?"

Rolland reflected back what he'd heard. "So I don't have to go in with a set plan for him. What I should actually do is hear out his thoughts and see what I can offer from my end to help him succeed even further with those ideas."

"That's it."

The two brainstormed solutions for a while longer before Rolland apologized again for interrupting Monroe's vacation. "I was hesitant to call," he said. "But I'm glad I did. I'll let you get back to your waves and sunshine."

Monroe signaled for the bar server to swing by and replace his watered-down cocktail. "Way ahead of you, my friend. Good luck."

ENRIQUE ARRIVED FOR THE MEETING WITH ROLLAND BEARING A SOMBER manner and an apology.

"Rolland," he said after sitting down, "I'm sure you've heard from Dom after I blew my cork with him. I want to apologize for that. He explained to me what you guys are looking to accomplish. I'm on board. The way you described it to me just set me off a little."

Rolland smiled; he hadn't known what to expect from the meeting, and he appreciated the outreach. "Listen, I didn't communicate my expectations well," he replied. "That's on me. I appreciate you and what you've had to say. I really will need your help. Dom is counting on us to pull through this. I appreciate your willingness to work with me."

The air cleared, Enrique's usual happy demeanor returned. "Hey, you know I'm here for my boys. And I really respect what you've been doing here as a manager and I want to support the team any way I can. If assisting with their sales is the best thing for Arachnid, count me in. Do you have anything else in mind?"

Rolland sensed the opening he and Monroe had talked about.

"You're going to be a huge asset with the team," he told Enrique. "At the same time, Dom's looking for a significant sales turnaround in the short term. You're our steadiest and best closer. If we could get even a small percentage increase in your sales, that would make a huge difference overall with the results Dom wants. I'm wondering if you were to look back at what you've been doing over the past month or so and what you've been experiencing with clients, is there anything you could have changed that would have increased your sales?"

Enrique leaned back, relaxed. "You don't last in this business if you're not constantly thinking about ways to improve," he said. "You've reminded me several times about accounts that I've gotten distracted from because of other big opportunities that came along. Remember Cerner calling you that one time, asking about me because I hadn't checked in for a while?"

"I do," Rolland affirmed.

"That got me to thinking," Enrique said. "I need to make a more concentrated effort to get back in touch with my existing customers and make them feel like it's the good old days again when they had a rep that had enough time to really be there for them as a partner. Being so busy has been good, but it's also been bad. When I proactively go visit these customers, I magically get more opportunities out of them than if I wait for them to call me."

It was precisely what Rolland wanted to hear. He started to speak, but Enrique wasn't done.

"In fact," he went on, "I remember back—I think before you were even on board here, Rolland—this one time I walked into Jennings Media. Tim Jennings was the owner back then, a real firecracker, liked to play hardball. This guy couldn't go golfing without turning it into a bet, and next thing you know there's a thousand dollars on the line. I was in there and he was bragging about these new computers he'd seen that would allow his team to render video conversions in half the time. I looked at him and asked, 'How come you haven't brought these up with me yet? Are you just telling me this to rub it in my face that you're considering a different vendor?'

"He was caught off-guard and seemed clueless. 'You guys don't sell computers,' he said. 'At least not these ones, do you?' He was the kind of guy who thought everything he had was the best out there, so if you didn't push back on him he wouldn't give you the time of day. So I just laughed at him and sarcastically said,

'What do you think *full-service technology* is supposed to mean? Come on, Jennings, of course we've got that.' By the time I left, I'd gotten him to close the order and I captured his hardware business, not just his networking—might as well work with the vendor you know, right? They hadn't originally thought of us. Had I not happened to show up and be present that day, I wouldn't have gotten the sale."

"What a story!" Rolland marveled. "I think what I hear you saying is that if you were to intentionally plan to go visit your primary clients more proactively than you have been, you think that would net some more immediate sales."

"That's exactly right," Enrique said. "Captain Obvious." Enrique grinned at Rolland.

Rolland laughed, then went on. "So based on that, in addition to helping the team with their sales, it sounds like you would make a change to help increase sales as well. When I said something about activities, my goal really was that the whole team feels like we're all working toward a common objective of making changes and increasing sales. Would you be OK with sharing your change idea with them?"

"I see your angle, Rolland. I can see why that'd be important," Enrique said. "I'm fine with telling them about this."

"Thank you, Enrique. That's going to mean a lot. So, how many customers were you thinking of doing this with?"

"I was thinking of doing regular meetings every two weeks with five or six—" He paused, deep in thought. "Well, actually, there's probably ten or twelve customers I should put on this."

Rolland jotted notes on his pad. "So you've got a dozen customers you want to meet with on a more regular basis," he said. "That sounds really good. I'll bet you've probably intended to do that over the last several months and just gotten sidetracked. So how do you expect to ensure that actually happens now?"

Enrique thought for a moment and then admitted that he'd tried various processes, but that they'd always been difficult to implement and maintain. "I've been selling for many years," he insisted. "I'm sure I can figure it out again."

"I respect your confidence," Rolland replied. "At the same time, I'm curious if there could be a way to simplify the strategy. Would it be beneficial if you had a system that knew each time you reached out to a client? And then, if the *right* amount of time had passed based on their priority to you, it would remind you to follow up again. Would that be valuable?"

"Yes, if it was able to do that for just those twelve customers and *that's it*, I'd say it would be helpful," Enrique agreed. "I don't want it doing that for every one of my customers, though; that'll drive me crazy."

"Understood," Rolland said. "I'm happy to say we do have a system that can do just that. All it would require is for you put on your calendar any time you call on those twelve clients."

Enrique's cheerful demeanor took a bit of a hit. He tilted his head slightly and asked, "That's not the CRM system, is it, Rolland?"

Rolland nodded. "It's a part of it, yes. Does that sound so bad?"

Enrique fell silent for a moment, then spoke. "You know, if it can do what you're saying it can do and that's it, no more stuff other than that, I'd be willing to give it a try."

Rolland couldn't hide his surprise. "I'm delighted to hear that," he said. "One of the great things about the system is its flexibility. I wouldn't want it to hold you back. We will make sure only to use the parts that you find helpful."

"So, you're not going to turn this into my version of the competition and start monitoring how many follow-up calls I make each week, are you?" Resistance edged into Enrique's voice.

"Not at all," Rolland reassured him. "I'm not looking to monitor anything. Making the calls is completely up to you if you see value in doing so. All I'm bringing to the table is a very low-impact way of helping you track what you said you wanted to do. It's strictly designed to help you manage your VIP client relationships, which will benefit your sales.

"What I would like to track and report to the rest of the team, if you're willing, are the resulting sales that you indicate are directly associated with these proactive calls that you go on. You'll know, Enrique, whether it was a sale you would have gotten anyway versus a sale that, as you say, you wouldn't have gotten if you weren't present. I think it'd be helpful for the team to see that even some of your sales are attributed to a change you made."

Enrique nodded. "All right, Rolland. I'll give it a shot. I do believe I'll make sales because of this. And I agree, it would be helpful for the team to hear from me because they could model the idea with their own accounts."

The two men shook hands, and Enrique headed for the door. Before walking out, he turned back and said, "But don't tell Dom I'm doing this." He grinned big. He'd been vocal about his distaste for the CRM previously.

"You have a reputation to maintain, right?" Rolland asked, jokingly.

"Bingo."

As he walked away, Enrique reflected on his nephews, Dom and Carlos, and all they'd put on the line to succeed with Arachnid. *If updating my methods is best for the boys, then I'll bite the bullet,* he thought. *Besides, my grandkids will reap the benefits of any extra sales I make on my way out, so maybe this old dog can learn at least one new trick.*

He stopped off to see Sarah. "I'd like you to show me how to record my calls with a few of my clients into this dag-nab CRM calendar," he told her. "I know it's supposed to work with my phone, too. How does that work? Where will it show up when the CRM has a reminder for my calendar?"

"Of course, Enrique," Sarah said cheerfully. "I'd be happy to show you. First, we'll need the dates of your last appointments with each customer." Sarah went on to quickly demonstrate how simple it would be for Enrique to put his meetings into the calendar. She also told him that once the right amount of time passed for a particular client, he'd see a notification show up right on his phone screen.

As they finished up, he lowered his voice to a whisper and leaned in. "You understand you can't be telling Dom I'm using this, right?"

Sarah smiled. "Mum's the word," she whispered back.

LATER IN THE WEEK CAME A BRIGHT MORNING. THE ALARM WENT OFF, AND Enrique roused and stretched, waking his dormant muscles for the coming day. He picked up his smartphone and saw an alert: *Check in with St. Luke's.*

"Well, look at that," Enrique said aloud. Upon further reflection, he realized it had been a while since he'd touched base with one of his longtime clients. "That's easy enough."

Enrique got out of bed and started prepping for the day. In the shower, he thought about the subtlety of the CRM system. The alert hadn't been intrusive at all, just a nudge. If anything, he was thankful for the reminder and a little disappointed in himself that he'd let so much time pass with St. Luke's.

I'll call first thing when I get to the office, he thought.

N EARLY A WEEK LATER, ANOTHER NOTIFICATION BUZZED ENRIQUE'S PHONE. He took note of the client—Sprint—then tended to other calls he had planned. When a break in his schedule came, he called Karen, his point person at Sprint.

"Hi, Karen, it's Enrique at Arachnid. Just thought I'd circle around and see how everything is going. I noticed that there's a new software patch for that backup issue you all have been having. Would you like me to email you the release notes on that?"

"That would be great, Enrique. Thank you," she said. "I'm glad you called. I was thinking the other day about you. Interested in lunch this week?"

"Always interested in lunch," he said, laughing. He enjoyed his easy rapport with Karen; they were always friendly, but also always about business. He looked forward to hearing what was on her mind.

"How about Friday?" she asked.

"Friday it is."

When they hung up, Enrique felt a surge of wonder. Somewhere in the background, the CRM system had prompted him to reach out to a well-established client. One phone call later, he had a lunch meeting. Nothing financial had come of it yet, but that would come, he was confident. The point was that he'd told Rolland he wanted to be in regular contact with his top customers, and the process he'd put in place was helping him achieve that.

O N FRIDAY, ENRIQUE ROLLED UP AT HARVEST DELI, AN UNASSUMING LITTLE sandwich shop that served side salads rather than the usual chips or fries. He'd become partial to the place since his doctor cautioned him to be more intentional about his blood pressure.

Karen was already waiting outside the door. He'd been eager for the meeting all week, knowing this was where the CRM system's contributions to his new process might be quantified. He walked up, Karen stood, and they shared a warm handshake before heading inside.

Seated, Enrique resisted the urge to make it all about business; he figured whatever had prompted Karen to ask him to lunch would come up in due time.

"It's been a while," he said. "I'm looking forward to getting caught up."

"It has been," Karen agreed. "Three months. I checked my calendar."

"Three months! Let's not let that happen again. Tell me, how are your grandkids? I just saw mine Sunday. They're such angels."

Karen's face lit up at the question. "They're great. Joe is starting tee-ball next month."

"Tee-ball? Are you kidding me? Wasn't it just yesterday that you were showing me a picture of him in the bassinet?"

"Seems like it, doesn't it?"

Enrique had done business with Sprint for a couple decades—in fact, when Enrique connected Dom with Sprint, he'd given Arachnid its launching pad. Enrique had a good history with many on the team over there, Karen chief among them. They fell easily into a friendly discussion about family and shared friends.

They dug in to their lunches. Between bites, Karen asked, "What are Dom and Carlos up to lately? Any exciting new visions?"

"As a matter of fact," Enrique said, "they've been putting significant development into expansion in Springfield."

"That's wonderful! New territory, new opportunities. It's a challenge, though, isn't it? We have a new trial concept for new corporate stores. We're opening four of them in Olathe to see how it works. Bill really has his hands full. The target opening dates are just two months out."

Enrique's ears perked up. This was the kind of opportunity he figured would turn up today. *So many services we could provide for an expansion like that,* he thought. He also knew he'd have to be subtle and not over-eager.

"Interesting," he said. "Will they all be serving neighboring areas of each other?"

"That's the plan," Karen said.

"So I take it they'll all be communicating and sharing information between sites. Has Bill thought about how to keep all of that data protected?"

Karen considered the question. "To be honest," she said, "I'm not sure. I know he's been focused on each location's individual needs, but he's not a network engineer. He might not have gotten around to how they'll interact. Would you have some ideas for him?"

150

Enrique dabbed the corners of his mouth with a napkin. "Well, sure. I'd be happy to help ease the process and make sure you guys have everything you need before opening."

"This is great, Enrique," Karen said. "I know he'd appreciate some time with you and would be open to ideas. I'll arrange for the two of you to be in the same room sometime next week."

"Sounds good."

"It's funny that you called," Karen mused. "Like I said, I'd been thinking about you and Arachnid, but then other things came up that demanded my attention. When I heard your voice, it got me thinking about how you could potentially help out with this."

They chatted some more. Enrique closed out the check, and then they walked to the parking lot together. "I'll have a date and time to you by the end of Monday about the meeting with Bill," Karen said. "Thanks for lunch. Have a great weekend."

As Enrique drove back to Arachnid, he sang along with the radio, his voice at top volume. It'd been too long since he'd been out to lunch with Karen, and it was as if nothing had changed. They had a good friendship and professional understanding, so it was reassuring to know that he could pick back up where he left off as long as he kept reaching out. *I'm going to have lunch appointments each day next week with one of my contacts*, he thought.

B ACK AT THE OFFICE, ROLLAND AND ENRIQUE SAT DOWN FOR A PLANNED follow-up from their previous meeting. As Enrique started spilling details from his lunch with Karen and the way the CRM system had worked with his new process to facilitate it, Rolland recognized that a true Post-Call Debrief was in order.

"Enrique, I'm thrilled to hear that the calendar notifications are working for you and prompting real action," he said. "Do you mind if we do a Post-Call?"

"Not at all," Enrique replied. "I think it's appropriate. There might be something more in there we can take away. It was just an excellent lunch, like old times with a trusted friend. We had some small talk, caught up, talked some shop, and I got the inside scoop on some expansion going on at Sprint. I have to give you credit, Rolland. I don't know what will come from next week's meeting with the project manager, but I do know that if it weren't for our little initiative and the reminders, I wouldn't have even heard about it. I'm optimistic about the prospects."

"What did you pick up from Karen that has you optimistic?"

"Well, for starters, the fact that she looped me in on the project to begin with suggests I've got a leg up and she still considers me an asset," Enrique said.

"Relationships are valuable, there's no denying that," Rolland agreed. "At the same time, you said it's Bill's project, right? Karen's definitely going to get you in the room, so what did you hear that makes you confident we can meet Bill's needs?"

"Fair enough," Enrique said. "There were a few things I discovered. First she told me he has his hands full and probably hasn't considered how the locations will all interact. So he could use another set of hands, especially one that understands networks and security. She also said that they have a launch date two months away, which means Bill has an urgent timeline."

Enrique was thorough. He was naturally optimistic, as any salesperson would be, but he also recognized the difference between a red-hot opportunity and a cloud of smoke. Rolland wasn't surprised. He simply wanted to keep Enrique tuned into the facts of the deal rather than any emotional aspects associated with a lighthearted lunch. He asked, "Do you know if Bill is already working with a local team? He might not be an engineer himself, but I wonder if he has some advisors around him."

"That would be good to know. You're right," Enrique conceded. "I should reach out to Karen again and learn what more I can. Since she offered to set the appointment, I never really took the time to clarify what I was expecting for next steps and what the agenda would look like with Bill. Thanks for the tip. I appreciate it." From there, Enrique talked through the rest of his intentions and goals related to the upcoming call.

Rolland wrapped up the meeting with a question: "Would you mind sharing your experience with the team on Monday? I think what you've accomplished is an excellent case study on successful and proactive account management. What's more, even though you aren't participating in the Discovery documentation competition, the questions you did ask really demonstrated what we're looking to have the others do. They would benefit from a quick training on the matter."

Enrique laughed. "I'd be happy to share it. I guess I'll have to cop to using the CRM system, huh? I always expected that word would eventually get out about that," he said. "At least this way it's on my own terms."

THE WEEKEND WENT BY IN A FLASH—THE ENTIRE MANDAT FAMILY HAD accompanied Allison on another college visit—and now Rolland finished the last of his preparations before 10 a.m. and the weekly sales-team meeting. He'd taken Monroe's advice to make the meetings into regular kickoffs to the week; before that, they had been irregular, disjointed affairs. Now, they rippled with energy. Rolland expected more of the same today, now that the team was several weeks into the activity challenge.

Rolland entered the conference room and invited everybody to get comfortable, grab a donut and some coffee, and get started.

"As is customary," he said, "let's start with our Success Roll Call. You all should have written up your achievements from the past week. Who wants to start?"

Diane, the newest member of the team, hopped right up. "I do!" she chimed. "First, though, I want to thank everybody for their patience and help while I've been working through the onboarding material. In the midst of all the training, I landed my first new customer, Pines Manufacturing. Not the biggest deal ever, but it feels good to start here at Arachnid by landing a new account."

A big "woot!" went up, and Enrique, Dom, Brad, Janet, and Rolland all congratulated her. They recognized the meaning of the deal for Diane. She was off and running, and Arachnid was reaping the rewards.

"That's excellent," Rolland said. "Who's next?" Everybody had something of import to share, whether a new deal, the expansion of an existing one, or a breakthrough in outreach to a desired client. Rolland was pleased.

"OK, everybody," Rolland said now. "Dom has an update on our sales metrics that he'd like to share."

Dom stood and faced the group. "Thank you, Rolland. Each of you has been turning up your performance these past few weeks, and I want to commend you for that. Two weeks ago, we stood at only eighty percent of the same quarter's performance a year ago. Now, we're up to ninety-five percent. We have lofty expansion goals, and if we continue to see this kind of turnaround, I have no doubt that we'll realize those goals. The significant uptick in Discovery meetings has translated into the technical team being busier developing quotes with sales engineering. Carlos is pleased, and so am I. Great work, everybody. Let's keep it up."

Rolland looked around the room. Every face was aglow and

smiling. He knew that the words of praise from the boss had made a deep impression. He felt the spark, too. A month ago, he'd been out of answers, ringing Monroe in Europe and begging for help. Now, they were on the brink of something big.

Rolland took the floor again. "Thank you for that, Dom. We appreciate it, and we're going to keep pushing hard. Next up, I wanted to have a little training segment in our meeting. Enrique is going to tell you about one of his successes and the takeaways from it." He motioned for Enrique to stand, giving his star salesman an impish grin. "He's also offered to give you all a demonstration on the use of the CRM system. Enrique, the floor is yours."

A murmur traveled through the room. Everybody—except, perhaps, Diane—knew that Enrique was no fan of the CRM.

Enrique, perhaps sensing the confusion, joked, "It's true, everybody. Today, I'm going to advocate for the fancy machine." He now looked at Dom, shaking a finger at his nephew. "But I'm not doing any demonstrations. Don't get me going on that."

A wave of laugher cascaded through the room.

Enrique cleared his throat and started in. "Several weeks ago, Sarah helped me configure calendar updates on my phone. The goal was to give me help identifying the frequency and consistency with which I was contacting some of my VIP clients. I'd gotten busy and allowed too much time to pass by with some of them. None of us are immune to the Tyranny of the Urgent. It's our natural instinct to attend to whatever project makes the most noise. I wanted a plan for staying on track with goals and proactively reallocating my time."

Enrique's plainspoken words had impact on the others. Certainly, Rolland and Dom, as leaders, commanded respect, but Enrique was the champion seller in the room; his words had a golden quality for the younger reps.

Enrique went on to explain the significance of account management and how without proactively scheduling his lunch with Sprint, he might never have gotten the chance to sell them on the new network security project. He also shared how part of his process was to define different categories that his customers fell into in order to help him prioritize who he should call more often. He differentiated his VIPs between the "A-pluses" and the "A-minuses."

"Once I remembered to set the meetings, my next issue was how to handle the conversations," Enrique continued. "While it's easy to reach out and discuss items about maintaining relationships, I really wanted these meetings to also be productive. I wanted to bring value to it—the sales equivalent of bringing a bottle of wine to a party. Before I reached out to Karen at Sprint, I found some information that she and her team needed, and I passed that on. At lunch, once we transitioned from small talk to her telling me about Sprint's situation, I used BANTC-related questions to drive that process."

As he explained his line of questioning with Karen, the rest of the team was attentive and asked a few insightful questions of their own. While Rolland sat and watched, he could only smile. He recognized that this was the first time Enrique had really engaged the team as a true mentor.

Enrique wrapped up and went to take his seat back. As he passed, Rolland shook his hand in gratitude for Enrique's willingness to try something new and then train the team on it.

"Speaking of the challenge," Rolland announced, "it's time to review the Jitter Board!" Jitter Board was the name he'd come up with because the challenge revolved around coffee cards in its current form.

"Brad," he said, "I'm pleased to see you turning the corner with your activity level. I'd be willing to bet it's only a matter of time before you start seeing closed sales as a result." Rolland pivoted. "Janet, you're currently in the lead, just like you told me you'd be. But don't get complacent—Diane is right on your heels! She's been holding quality Discovery meetings non-stop. In fact, those actions played a large role in landing Pines."

After imparting where they all stood with the competition, Rolland gave everyone a couple of minutes at the end of the meeting to write down the one thing that was going to be the most important for them to focus on during the week ahead. He encouraged them to share their goals with each other and collaborate if possible in order to meet more goals as a team.

"Remember, we have a focus on near-term goals, and Enrique and I are available to partner with you on sales," Rolland said. "I heard all of your goals, and I didn't hear any of them specifically say you wanted to take advantage of that. I'd recommend considering where we can contribute and then looping us in."

Enrique spoke up. "I'd like to add to that, Rolland. You guys have access to the two of us, who have been involved in selling here for a combined twenty-plus years. Leveraging that experience by bringing us along on your sales calls is really going to make a difference for you. And like Rolland said, you should make it a point to engage with us *this* week on something."

Rolland smiled as he watched his veteran fire up the team. Not only was Enrique a part of the group and its success, but he'd also completed the transition into his role as a mentor and leader.

"Great point, Enrique," Rolland affirmed. "Lastly, if anybody needs to meet to review their individual progress and make adjustments to their plan, let me know. Otherwise, we all know what we're aiming for this week. Get out there and make it happen."

Takeaways

An Old Salesman's New Tricks

Coaching, Account Management, and Sales Team Meetings

A S A MANAGER IT MAY SEEM MORE NATURAL TO GIVE DIRECTIVES THAN TO take a seat and listen. However, salespeople in the Service Balloon like Enrique require more tact. It's like Monroe said, "Coaching, just like how accountability partnerships work, differs from one salesperson to the next."

Can you identify the best coach you ever had, whether personal, athletic, or professional? What were the qualities and characteristics that made them the best? Coaching is all about accentuating the skills, knowledge, and innate capabilities that your sales-team members have within them. The trick is knowing that not every salesperson will respond positively to the same coaching style.

"Coach" is a wonderful blanket title that people use when describing how they interact with others as an expert. Whether you teach in a classroom, manage an Olympic volleyball team, provide personal or professional consulting, train gym-goers, or write an advice column, it would be easy and acceptable in most circles to say you "coach." However, when you observe the coach of a kindergarten soccer program essentially herding cats, how are they coaching? There are big differences between them and how a golf pro engages with their students on the driving range.

The Coaching Spectrum

WHEN SO MANY DIFFERENT KINDS OF COMMUNICATION CAN FALL UNDER the umbrella of coaching, you need to understand when each style helps you succeed with each member of your team. ISM uses five different types of coaching, from telling to listening, in what is called the Coaching Spectrum.

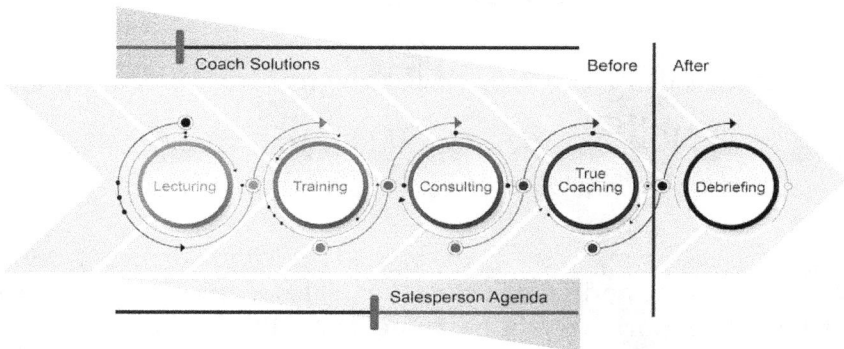

Coaching Spectrum™

Download a full-sized color copy of the Coaching Spectrum by accessing this book's Companion Resource website—www.acultureofpredictablesales.com.

Rolland was working from the left side of the Spectrum during his meetings with Brad, from a pure telling position of Lecture to a Training style as Brad demonstrated cooperation. Before going to Enrique, however, he should have recognized that he needed to begin on the right-hand side of the spectrum, listening through Debriefing, and move toward the left as Enrique invited him to do so. Noting the differences in style and levels of responsibility in your salespeople will help you figure out where on the Coaching Spectrum you should begin and continue with them.

At the **Lecture** and **Train** positions, you will dictate the focus areas much as a professor determines a class syllabus. Essentially, you're downloading your brain for the salesperson to absorb and apply. With Lecturing, you don't find out if the material was grasped and understood until a "test" event occurs and the salesperson either passes or fails. As a manager, avoid going this far left on the spectrum unless it's a situation similar to laying out non-negotiable corporate rules across the entire department.

The main difference with Training is that you check in to gauge how well the material makes sense to the trainee. You maintain control of the talking points, but there's more interaction. Any time you're training a less-experienced salesperson in a new skill, it's helpful to ask questions to validate their comprehension and then role-play or implement other application practices.

> Lecturing differs from Training in that it only ensures exposure to information, whereas Training ensures digestion and understanding.

We saw a good example of this when Enrique was in front of the team during their Sales Team Meeting. While he had full control over the discussion, he also asked others to share their thoughts. In Lecturing, we ensure that the audience has been *exposed* to what they need to know. In Training, we attempt to ensure that they've *digested* and fully understood what they need to know.

Only then do we consider whether we've been successful. You would tend to use these approaches with less-experienced salespeople who would acknowledge they have things they need to learn; where their perspective is that you know something they do not that it would be beneficial for them to understand.

From the middle of the spectrum to the right, the salesperson should begin identifying what topics they need help with and work cooperatively with you to brainstorm solutions. In **Consulting**, you continue to be the expert with the knowledge and the salesperson accesses your knowledge when and how they desire to do so. The change here is that they initiate their own learning. Consulting is more cooperative and less academic. As such there is a greater expectation that the salesperson will execute on what they've learned. Consulting tends to be the position on the spectrum where many managers are most comfortable because they are able to put their fingers into the business personally in a way that is reactive to the requests of their salesperson. This is also because Consulting continues to assume that the primary source of know-how comes from the one providing the consulting (i.e. the manager).

True Coaching turns control over to the salesperson to both identify their needs *and* determine the solution. This transitions from cooperation to service, so it's often very appropriate when working with Service Balloon salespeople. Your role is primarily to interact with the salesperson and assist them in connecting the dots between the needs they've recognized and the solutions they can identify. Performing True Coaching can be difficult for you as a manager because you are essentially relinquishing your role as the sole source of knowledge. It also means you're trusting that the salesperson is innately capable of solving their own needs.

There's a parallel here to parenting. At some point, your kids become old enough to make decisions for themselves. You have to step back and trust they'll make the best decision without consulting you on every issue. If you've ever watched *The Voice*, the judges on the show are excellent examples of true coaches. The contestants arrive with a natural ability to sing. Some may have had formal training. Either way, the coaches aren't there to teach them how to sing. They're there to say things like, "What if you tried singing it this way?" or "You can own that note!" I couldn't tell you what it means to "own a note," but the contestants seem to understand it and are able to demonstrate a marked change.

The key to True Coaching is to use questions as your primary tool without putting your employee on the defensive. While Consulting is where managers are most comfortable, True Coaching is what they should strive to do most often.

Managers often feel most comfortable Consulting, but should engage in True Coaching instead.

Try to stay in True Coaching mode until it becomes obvious, to either yourself or the salesperson, that they *do not actually have* a desirable solution in their mind. That is an opening for you to shift back to Consulting just long enough to provide them with answers and then you can slide back to True Coaching. The initial assumption is that the salesperson has the solution but needs help connecting the dots to get them there. It's not until you figure out that you're reaching for something that doesn't exist that you switch from Coaching to Consulting.

With Service and upper-level Partner Balloon salespeople, it is a best practice to wait until the salesperson asks you for a solution before switching from True Coaching to Consulting. If you recall from the mentoring takeaways, it's critical that you move between levels *with* your protégé rather than advancing ahead of them and pulling them along without checking to see if they are open and comfortable. Similar rules apply when you're moving left to right in the spectrum with a weaker salesperson. Just like how the Balloon Model suggests you increase the time you invest in an Assess Balloon salesperson based on the demonstration of their desire to improve and develop, you should also modify the Coaching Spectrum style you use based on observed growth and feedback from the salesperson.

There are times that even top salespeople require some formal training, such as Enrique with the CRM system. Even then, it's important to only shift to the training portion of the spectrum when invited to by your salesperson. Be careful—if a Service Balloon salesperson asks for training, it's likely that what they really want is for you to Consult with them (i.e., they will explain to you what they want to know more about and you will help them). Rarely do they want you to put together the agenda and present to them—or even worse, lecture them on the topic.

Debriefing is a tool with a unique purpose. While True Coaching, and the positions to the left of it, tend to focus on the present or future, Debrief focuses on the past—usually a specific event. When salespeople don't meet minimum-results expectations, you need to take more control over defining the agenda, setting targets, and dictating strategy. On the other hand, the last thing you want to do is offend a 30-year sales veteran in the Service Balloon by putting them in a formal training setting where the implicit message is that they don't know how to sell.

Therefore, from a coaching perspective, you'd start at Debriefing, where you observe their actions and discussing what is working for them and what is not. As the Service salesperson opens the door to a deeper discussion, you can move slowly to the left on the spectrum and provide them with more direct feedback about best practices they may not have considered or known. Remember that with every position on the spectrum from True Coaching back to Lecturing, the discussion focuses on *informing* the audience before action is taken.

A common mistake is using Post-Call Debrief meetings to Lecturing and/or Train.

A Debrief happens after a call is completed: "Did we get the results we wanted?" and "Why do you think we didn't?" and "What can be learned?" Aside from the timing, debriefing is just like True Coaching in that you engage with questions to help connect the dots, but the ideas and solutions all come from the salesperson.

A common mistake is for managers to see debrief meetings as a platform to Lecture/Train. They might recognize an error and assume that since the error exists, it's an open invitation to submit their ideas and solutions on the subject. That's not how it's supposed to work, though. More success comes when the Coaching Spectrum style is matched to the salesperson and situation that you are working with.

In the last chapter, Rolland started with Enrique by delivering his own agenda because he was stuck in that rut after working with Janet, Brad and Diane. But after talking to Monroe, Rolland stepped back and when he prompted the thought process, Enrique identified his own area of improvement—Account Management. From there, Rolland allowed Enrique to work through possible solutions. It wasn't until Enrique grasped the flaws in his plan and had a willingness to listen that Rolland submitted his own idea—to use the CRM. When a salesperson is in your Service Balloon, coaching is mostly about lending an ear and "moving the mountains out of their way."

To successfully implement these coaching approaches, start by choosing your strategy from the spectrum based upon what you know about the beliefs and expectations of each salesperson. Then, in coaching sessions with them, start with things that are positive and build, *only as invited,* toward constructive feedback and discussion. Only from a strong foundation of trust with your team will you be able to create Accountability Partnerships that can result in real positive change.

Account Management

ENRIQUE IDENTIFIED ACCOUNT MANAGEMENT AS AN AREA HE WANTS TO improve. While the rest of the team focuses on closing new customers, Enrique can better tap his book of current customers. Maintaining relationships with current accounts increases your residual income and gives you opportunities to upsell. Building and maintaining customer loyalty needs to be at the heart of the sales strategy.

Even with customers who are in frequent contact and regularly place orders, there should be an emphasis on cultivating each relationship and bringing the customer closer to your company. Your sales team needs a plan for reaching out to current clients and adding value to their day "just because" to strengthen relationships. I call this behavior "making deposits." You have to first make a deposit into a bank account before you can withdraw money. The same principle applies with customer accounts. If you don't maintain positive interactions with them, your account will be empty when the time comes for you to ask for more.

> Sales teams need to have a proactive plan to strengthen relationships and add value to their clients' day 'just because.'

Maintaining current relationships can be difficult because it requires an ongoing investment of time for the hope of a future return. It's much easier to tend to whichever hinge squeaks the loudest or, as Enrique put it, fall victim to the "Tyranny of the Urgent." Enrique needed a plan for staying on track with goals and proactively reallocating his time." He recognized the value in account management but had allowed himself to get busy and distracted with other projects. In my experience, this is common among Service-level, highly experienced salespeople.

So, what does a proactive Account Management plan look

like? It begins with identifying high-value customers. Enrique's approach was to focus on his top ten to twelve VIP clients and to differentiate his level of investment with each based on whether they were "A-pluses" or "A-minuses." ISM has a similar technique for evaluating customers called the Account Management Matrix.

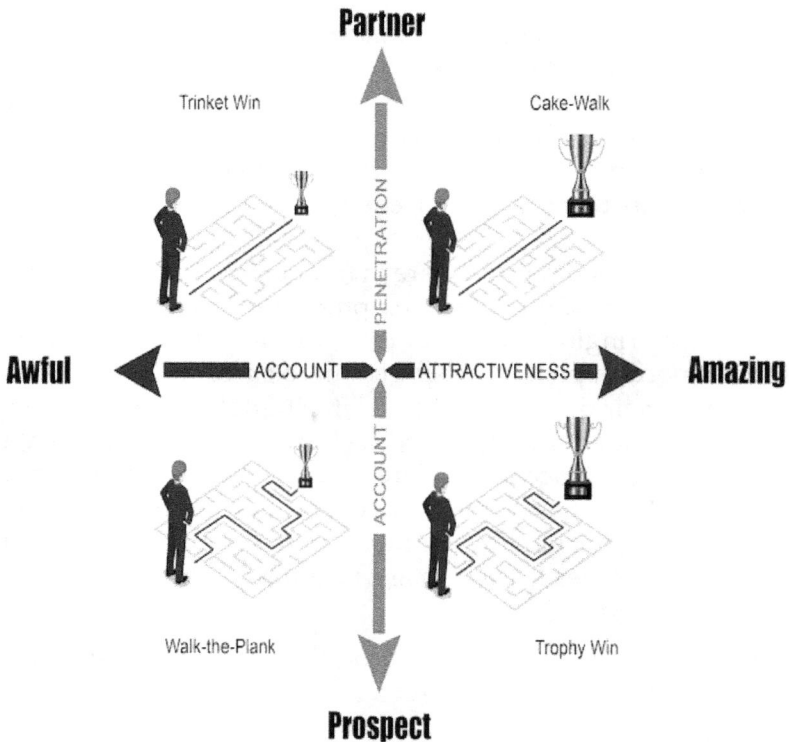

Account Management Matrix™

Download a full-sized color copy of the Account Management Matrix by accessing this book's Companion Resource website—www.acultureofpredictablesales.com.

THE MATRIX HAS TWO PERPENDICULAR AXES. THE HORIZONTAL AXIS MEASures "Attractiveness" and ranges from Awful to Amazing. **Attractiveness** could be based on factors such as customer location, budget, serviceable area, etc. and how well those factors align with your company's target demographic. The key here is to understand what characteristics indicate highly profitable and desirable customers. Not all customers and prospects are created equal. The vertical axis measures "Penetration" and ranges from Prospect to Partner. **Penetration** refers to how deeply your company has been able to capture a customer's business and mindshare. For instance, a Partner company would not only buy 100 percent of the products and services you sell, from you, but would also involve you at a strategic level in their company planning and regularly provide you significant referrals.

Which quadrant a customer falls into will determine the level of investment that a salesperson should commit toward managing their account. A customer in the Amazing/Partner quadrant would fit Enrique's "A-minus" criteria because they have a great relationship and benefit from Arachnid's services, but they're already being serviced to capacity. He would rather spend a large chunk of his time making deposits with the "A-plus" customers in the Amazing/Prospect quadrant. Of course, current accounts are not technically prospects, but the quadrant suggests Arachnid hasn't yet captured all of their potential business.

Identifying high-value customers is a great first step, but how does your salesperson plan to engage with them? Enrique chose to make check-in calls and then, if possible, transition into a lunch meeting. It's important to match the investment of time and energy with the quadrant a client fits into in order to maximize the ROI of a salesperson's account-management efforts.

> Establish monthly action and outreach objectives in the account management plan to help avoid procrastination.

Going out for lunch each day, as Enrique boldly proclaimed, would take a lot of time from his other responsibilities. But if that investment of time is most likely to bring the highest ROI of sales out of his account book, then more power to him. The biggest opportunities deserve the biggest time and resource deposits. It's still important to reach out to smaller opportunities as well, but in different ways—like a phone call or email—or perhaps less often. It's all about positioning yourself to have top-of-mind-awareness (TOMA) with your customers.

After a salesperson has organized their client list into the quadrants and determined what actions to take with each, the next steps are to develop a checklist and execute that plan. At the same time, they should adapt to client feedback (was the activity accepted or rejected?) and service realities (do the scheduled activities make sense given recent interactions that already took place?) over time.

In the past, Enrique had tried to use a calendar to keep track of all these efforts. But, now he'll try the CRM system. You're likely to see the best results when the schedule of best-practice activities is readdressed or prepared on a quarterly basis with monthly objectives. Often, the schedules of the salesperson and, more importantly, the client don't allow for the activities to take place *exactly* as planned.

By providing the flexibility of an entire month to accomplish each activity, if there's intent to follow through, the salesperson and their client will usually be able to find an aligned time. Be aware that without monthly objectives, the actions and outreach tend to be procrastinated to the last days of the quarter, which will make it more difficult for the client to fit the salesperson into their schedule. These actions have a greater impact when they fit in smoothly with the client's natural interactions with the company.

Post-Call Debriefs

AFTER YOUR SALESPEOPLE GO OUT ON CALLS, PART OF COACHING THEM IS TO ensure that they are properly interpreting how their conversations went and what next steps are appropriate. After Enrique's lunch with Karen, we observed Rolland conduct **a Post-Call Debrief** meeting with him. This is an important meeting to hold with salespeople any time they get back from a high-value call with critical next steps. Doing so as soon after the call as possible means the details will be fresh in the salesperson's memory. You want to hear the most accurate details as possible because the goals of a Post-Call Debrief are:

» To understand what the salesperson learned or accomplished during the call
» To gain clarity for resulting deal strategy with the salesperson
» To identify any lessons that the salesperson can benefit from in the future

To best achieve those goals, a typical Post-Call Debrief follows a five-point agenda in the ISM system:

» **Gain an Understanding**: where you get clarity on what actually happened
» **What Went Well**: where you identify things that went well, those that didn't, and what can be improved on
» **Identify Deltas**: where you look at whether any BANTC elements have changed
» **Execution Review**: where you talk about how well the salesperson executed their game plan
» **Lessons Learned and Next Steps** where you talk about the outcomes of the call, what can be learned, and what to do next

Let's look at each of these in more detail.

Gaining an understanding of the call gives you a chance to get up to speed on the deal since you may have many other coaching situations that you handle daily. While listening to the salesperson's recap, keep in mind what the original goals of the call were. Salespeople have a tendency to morph the strategies in their mind, much like the game of Telephone. They knew the original plans, but in trying to remember the specifics of a call, they can twist the plans in their mind and become convinced that the changes that actually occurred were part of the original plan. You don't want them to lose sight of the intended strategies and targets.

The **What Went Well** portion categorizes different aspects of the call into "what went especially well," "what didn't work at all," and "what can be improved on." This is a practice in evaluation, yet it maintains a sense of positivity. It's always motivational to identify what went especially well, so you won't have much trouble getting the salesperson to participate. When it comes to "what didn't work at all," almost all of what a salesperson is likely to identify can be spun back to them as something that actually fits in the final category, "what can be improved on."

Rarely does an action qualify as "didn't work at all," which actually motivates the salesperson once they realize that category is empty. It's like a sudden wave of relief because they were met with optimism and understanding when they thought they were admitting failure. The conversation will naturally transition into what can be improved on, which is where the coaching takes place.

From there, it's important to dissect the facts of the call in order to **Identify Deltas**. What was specifically said that would indicate a shift, forward or backward, in any of the BANTC factors? (Remember that BANTC is **Budget**—how willing a prospect is to take tradeoffs to accomplish their goals; **Authority**—how sure are we that we have strong advocacy from all relevant parties to purchase from us; **Needs** —what emotional level does the prospect feel about their needs that we can uniquely address; **Timeframe**—what costs and problems will occur if the prospect waits longer to make a decision; and **Credibility**—why and how strongly does the customer feel about including you in the buying process.)

You aren't evaluating the salesperson's understanding of BANTC, but rather determining whether the client shared any significant information in any one of the categories that would warrant advancing the sale to the next stage. This is where reality meets the optimism of the salesperson. It's important that the two of you cooperatively decide whether the sale is going to advance.

> Post Call Debrief meetings are where reality meets the optimism of the salesperson.

After establishing the intent of the call, what went well according to that plan, and what deltas occurred in relation to BANTC, it's time for the **Execution Review**. This is no longer about the sale itself, but rather how well the salesperson executed their game plan. Are there any techniques and selling abilities they can improve on?

There are a few specific focus areas for this conversation. To begin with, how convincingly was the *client invited* into the call? The best case is always for the client to have a compelling incentive for taking the call in the first place. It's also a good idea to clarify whether the salesperson openly *shared the agenda* for the call in order to manage the client's expectations. Even during his lunch meeting, Enrique made sure to tell Karen how he was just looking to catch up, but he'd be open to discussing new opportunities if the possibility existed. If a salesperson doesn't state their intentions upfront and agree to an agenda with the client, the client is likely to be spending the meeting waiting for whatever bomb is going to be dropped on them.

After the salesperson has put the client at ease by clarifying the agenda, the next question is how well they *maintained that level of comfort* throughout the call. How well was the background of the call received? Was the client engaged and open to continuing the conversation? This reveals whether the salesperson was *pushing* the sale along or being *pulled* by the client.

It may seem negative at first, but being "pulled" doesn't mean being run over or dragged. It means the client was fully interested in advancing the sale and couldn't get to the next stage fast enough. If a salesperson has to constantly push, then the deal is less likely to ever close.

The final focus area addresses how well the salesperson *clarified the next steps* with the client. Every meeting that consists of movement, whether it was positive or negative, should end with a discussion of next steps. Success depends on how well it's understood who has the ball in their court. When reviewing the salesperson's execution, a question like, "What actions did you take to make sure the client understood and agreed with what next steps would be taken?" can quickly reveal the facts.

The Post-Call Debrief concludes with a brief discussion of **Lessons Learned and Next-Step Strategies**. It is a great tool for learning and holding people accountable to the execution of their plans. Recognizing mistakes and understanding what can be done differently is crucial to the development of any professional, especially in sales. Pay attention to these learning points—they can serve as useful training topics to include in your Sales Team Meeting, as Rolland demonstrated.

Sales Team Meetings

SALES TEAM MEETINGS ARE AN EXCELLENT WAY TO KICK OFF A WEEK BEcause their primary goal is motivation. If this isn't the case for your weekly team meeting, change the agenda so that it is. These 30 to 45 minutes are a great opportunity to share highlights such as major sales and promotions, or to discuss a roadblock that was overcome. Salespeople go out all week long being told "No, no, no" and chasing customers who hide and lie to them. This meeting is designed to energize the sales team by reviewing the previous week's accomplishments and preparing them mentally for the week ahead.

Sales team meetings are one of the most frequently misunderstood and mismanaged meetings. Managers often fail to understand that when you bring the whole team together, the goal should be motivation, and not much else. Frequently, the meeting becomes more about themselves. Since they have their whole team in one place, they focus on getting caught up on certain deals and providing public coaching so as to save their own time. This has the opposite effect on salespeople. Instead, this meeting needs to be a place where they can rejuvenate and feel confident that they are a part of something successful.

Rolland's first team meeting at the beginning of this book looked just like one of those mismanaged events. He didn't follow an agenda and he allowed his team to redirect the conversation toward problems without solutions and finger-pointing rather than keeping on track with his intended message of "Now is our time!" However, in his second Sales Team Meeting he stuck to the ISM agenda that he'd learned from Monroe. Sales Team Meetings have fairly standard opening and closing bookends with a more flexible middle.

This is the Agenda recommended by the ISM System:

» **Success Roll Call**
» **Key Metrics Overview**
» **Management Structured Success Story (optional)**
» The middle can be flexible, potentially including:

  • **Salesperson Testimonial**
  • **Training** – that is relevant to the whole group
  • **Company Focused Corner**

» **Collaborative Discussions**
» **Goal Setting**

Let's look at how Rolland utilized this format. At the onset, Rolland conducted a **Success Roll Call**—in which everyone wrote down their past week's successes and then some shared them with the group—and then he had Dom share a **Key Metrics Overview** that highlighted as many positive outcomes as possible. If you find yourself with key metric results that aren't so good, it's still important to share them because seeing the scoreboard can impact competitive salespeople, and it helps everyone understand goals and standards they need to be working toward.

When Key Metrics aren't where they should be, just limit your comments about them. The final part of the opening is the **Management**

Structured Success Story. This is an optional piece in which you can arrange to have a salesperson share a Success Roll Call story in greater depth. Rolland skipped this because he'd already planned to have Enrique share a success later in the meeting. During your one-on-one meetings with your salespeople, listen for stories that you can use during this time—most people love to share their successes.

While Diane did share a quick success, the difference between hers and Enrique's presentation is that Rolland asked Enrique ahead of time to elaborate on the problem they were facing, the solution they implemented, and their results. When salespeople hear what success their peers are achieving, they start to think, "I can too." The opening of your Sales Team Meeting should focus on motivation by creating positivity, inspiring success, and communicating attainability.

The meeting's middle is flexible and depends on your team's needs in a given week. Mostly it is used to further inspire success and affect group focus. You might include a short training demonstration that will turn the team's attention to a specific matter. Better yet, bring in an expert or have one of your salespeople share a success. By example, Rolland asked Enrique to share his implementation of CRM to improve his Account Management. The most valuable part of Enrique's training was that it was empowering to the others; they felt as if they'd received a new tool.

> In Sales Team Meetings, avoid discussions that benefit only one salesperson while the others fall asleep.

You could alternatively fill this portion of the meeting with a discussion about a new trend that's surfacing in the marketplace or within your company. Do you now have access to a new product line? Is the company making strides toward an impressive achievement? The ISM system refers to this section as the **Company Focused Corner**. The Company Focused Corner can be filled with anything designed to inspire your team to succeed and focus them on a particularly desirable objective. Keep housekeeping items short and relevant to all. Sales Team Meetings should not be used to address matters of accountability, team failures, or policy changes that will be perceived as negative. These all go against the grain of the meeting's motivational goal. Avoid one-on-one strategy discussions that benefit only you, or a single salesperson, while everyone else falls asleep. Remember that each person in attendance needs to be gaining value from every minute of the meeting.

The closing bookend focuses on **Collaborative Discussions** and **Goal Setting.** Salespeople are naturally independent, but there are times when multiple people or even a whole department is facing a similar hurdle. Unless an issue that affects everyone is discussed openly in this type of setting, salespeople may perceive that they are alone in their struggles.

Let's look at an example from the Company Focused Corner above; a new product line. While it's an exciting new initiative, perhaps it has also exposed your salespeople to a new competitor. In their minds, they have to figure out how to win bids over this competitor on a case-by-case basis, which is intimidating to take on alone. Having an open discussion about it will allow your whole team to collaborate and determine what differentiates your offering from competitors, empowering individual salespeople to bid confidently.

Moderating a collaborative discussion allows each person who has a stake in the matter to bring forward ideas that someone else may not have considered yet. This creates a sense of camaraderie and generates more creative solutions to roadblocks that were impeding progress. Just make sure your topic is small enough that the collaboration can be done in a few minutes; otherwise a separate meeting should be scheduled for interested parties.

The final part of a Sales Team Meeting is **goal setting,** because it ends the meeting with everyone focusing on something important. The emphasis here is on the *one* thing that they absolutely have to achieve in the next week to position them for success. Rolland not only had his team write down their goals, he also had them share their goals aloud with one another. This practice increases each salesperson's likelihood of achieving their goals because everyone else will know if they don't. Enrique stepped up as a peer leader during this time by pointing out how the rest of the team could leverage his and Rolland's willingness to co-sell on a few of their deals to help them reach their own goals faster.

The Weekly Sales Team Meeting is your chance to energize your team all at once and guide them going into the week ahead. By keeping the mood positive, your team will feel rejuvenated, have a proper course charted for them, and be committed to achieving both personal and team success. Coaching and Motivation, combined with effective meetings are crucial driving forces of the Support wall of the Team Balloon Model—and ultimately, the success of your team. The entire ISM system is about meeting each salesperson where they are at and leveraging your interactions with them to enhance your ability to influence their growth and realize greater results.

Overview of the Concepts in This Chapter

» **Coaching Spectrum**

- **Lecture** – you determine the agenda and action items
- **Train** – you determine the agenda and action items while also testing the salesperson's level of understanding
- **Consult** – the salesperson determines when and what they need to learn from you
- **Coach** – the salesperson is afforded the opportunity to dictate their own learning as well as their own outcomes; your role to help them connect the dots by asking the right questions
- **Debrief** – this is coaching that takes place after action has already been taken; like reviewing the game film for what could be improved

» **Account Management**

- Tyranny of the Urgent – salespeople that lack a proactive plan will tend to the hinge that squeaks the loudest
- **Step 1:** Identify High Value Customers Using the Account Management Matrix
  - ◦ Attractiveness - Awful to Amazing
  - ◦ Penetration - Prospect to Partner
- **Step 2:** Inventory Best Practice Service Activities (Deposits)
- **Step 3:** Develop a schedule of deposits for the Sales Team to perform
- **Step 4:** Proactively Execute the Plan and Adapt to Feedback

» **Post-Call Debrief**

- **Gain an understanding** of the sale
- **Hear 'What went well'** as well as what can be improved upon
- **Identify Deltas** – were there significant shifts in BANTC?
- **Execution Review** – evaluate the salesperson's techniques
  - ◦ Invited in
  - ◦ Agenda Set / Review
  - ◦ Background Reception
  - ◦ Push / Pull Evaluation
  - ◦ Clarity of Next Steps
- **Identify Next Steps** based on lessons learned

» **Sales Team Meetings**

- Motivation is the primary focus
- Agenda
  - ◦ Success Roll Call
  - ◦ Key Metrics Overview
  - ◦ Management Structured Success Story
  - ◦ The middle can be flexible, potentially including:
    - □ Salesperson Testimonial
    - □ Training – that is relevant to the whole group
    - □ Company Focused Corner
  - ◦ Collaborative Discussions
  - ◦ Goal Setting

CHAPTER SIX

A Really Big Deal

ALMOST READY TO LEAVE THE APARTMENT, JANET STOPPED AT HER VI-sion board and took a deep gaze into it. Since joining Arachnid, she had made this a morning ritual, a way of getting into the right mindset for the day. Her eyes followed a path of magazine cutouts and words and images that held resonance for her: a hoped-for Hawaiian vacation, winning the Jitter Board contest at work, fitness goals. Days had a way of occasionally deviating from her intentions; mornings at the vision board brought her day into focus.

Today, a Tuesday, meant she would start with Pilates, one of the ways she was pursuing more rigorous physical activity. She also found the exercise mind-clearing, which helped with not only work but also her life as a whole.

After taking in the visuals, Janet fairly bounced out of her apartment, down the stairs and to her car.

UPON ENTERING THE GYM, JANET SPOTTED HER FRIEND JENNIFER. A pleasant surprise: She'd known Jennifer for years, as their families were close as the women grew up, and Jennifer had even once worked for Janet's father. In fact, it had been Jennifer who'd suggested Pilates to Janet, who'd taken to it with gusto but hadn't seen her friend at the gym in a long while.

"Great to see you, Jenny," Janet said. "Long time."

Jennifer smiled, dropping her shoulders to set her bag on the ground. "It's nice to be back. I've needed this."

"Busy, huh?"

"*Insanely*," Jennifer said. Her face lit up. "Did I even tell you about this? I got a new job."

"Really?"

"Yeah," Jennifer said. "Hallmark. The transition has been really intense, but on the bright side, it gave me some schedule flexibility so I can start making it here in the mornings. We'll be seeing more of each other, I guess."

"Great!" Janet said. "Hallmark—a great Kansas City company. Congratulations! You want to get some coffee after class? I'd love to hear more about it."

"I'd like that," Jennifer said. "Got a spot in mind?"

"Sure do!" Janet said, smiling. "I've been meaning to check out Perks Café. A lot of my friends have been saying good things about it. What do you think?"

"I haven't heard of it," Jennifer said. "But sounds good to me." She picked up her bag again.

"Excellent," Janet replied. "I'll text you the address. *After* I show you how it's done in here." Janet chuckled and gave Jennifer a friendly nudge as they headed off to the workout room.

L ATER, WHILE THEY WAITED IN LINE AT PERKS, JANET TOOK IN THE ATMOSPHERE. The café sat on a corner, with a chalkboard sign out front listing daily specials. Autumn was in the air and in the décor, with gourds and harvest vegetables filling baskets and deep, rich, earthy colors splashing the walls.

"I love coffee," Janet said. "Love, love, love. I've heard such great things about this place." She pointed to the menu board. "What do you think? The maple cinnamon-roll latte with almond milk? That sounds *delicious*."

"Sounds great," Jennifer said.

When they reached the front of the line, Janet placed the order for both of them and gave her name to the cashier.

"You don't have to do that, Janet," Jennifer said. "I can get my own."

"I invited you," Janet said. "My treat." She handed the cashier her card.

When their drinks arrived, Janet insisted on a selfie, with the two of them holding up their cups.

"I'm a mess," Jennifer protested. "That workout killed me."

"Just one picture," Janet pressed. "I have to show my friends that I finally made it here. It'll be fun."

Jennifer gamely leaned in, and they smiled for the picture. Janet's thumbs now raced to finish captioning and posting the photo to Facebook. "This will take just a minute," she said. "Fun!"

Once the photo was online, she turned her attention back to Jennifer.

"OK, tell me about Hallmark," she said. "That's so awesome. What's the job like?"

"Hard. Challenging. Rewarding," Jennifer said. "All the things I'd hoped it would be. I started in late August—you know, about the time I stopped showing up at the gym." She laughed, then took a sip of her latte. "This really *is* good."

"I know!" Janet said. "I'm definitely coming back."

"Anyway," Jennifer went on. "I'm the new director of ERP. Hallmark has been working with their original, homegrown accounting system, but they need to bring everything into the modern age. My job is basically to oversee that project and successfully move all their systems over to SAP, then oversee the system once we've made the conversion."

Janet cringed. She could see now why Jennifer had been so scarce. "That sounds like quite an ordeal, especially if they created a brand-new position for it."

Jennifer nodded. "The VP I report to expects it to take a few years to fully implement, given the size of the company and the scope of the project."

"Wow!" Janet said. "That sounds like a huge load to carry."

Jennifer took another sip of her coffee. "It is," she said, "but I'm excited to take it on. There will be several moving parts, which will challenge me, and at the same time, I'm learning so much that will really benefit my career going forward." Jennifer rested her elbows on the table and began touching her fingertips together as she listed responsibilities. "We'll need to move each subsidiary account over. We'll need to remap all of the processes and procedures so that the business systems support the executive reporting needs. We'll need the proper technology in place to operate all of it. Not to mention all of the training that will have to be done with each internal team so they are up to speed."

Janet marveled at the sheer size of the undertaking. "They've got the right person for the job, is all I can say," she said, toasting her friend. "I'm so happy for you. What an incredible opportunity."

"I appreciate it," Jennifer said. She then paused, letting the conversation reset. "How are things at Arachnid going for you?"

Janet sat up a bit straighter. "We've actually been in the middle of some major process changes as well. My boss is really tightening up the sales team, which I was admittedly skeptical of at the start."

Jennifer nodded. "Change can be scary like that."

"However," Janet said, seizing back her optimism, "it's been helping me stay on top of activities and keep deals moving forward efficiently. In fact, I'm scheduled to have an Activity Review meeting with him this morning."

"How are sales going?" Jennifer asked. "Are you making any money yet?"

Janet was impressed by the directness of the question. "Absolutely. Things are going well. I'm actually impressed with the tech team, and the companies I've gone into so far have all been thrilled with our service."

Jennifer looked pensively across the room, beyond Janet, before focusing on her again. "You know, since running into you at the gym, I've been bouncing around the idea of seeing if there's some way we could work together. I'm glad to hear companies are liking you and your team at Arachnid."

"That would be great," Janet said.

"Maybe there's something you could offer in terms of support on my conversion project," Jennifer mused. "Of course, I can't guarantee anything, and Hallmark probably has agreements with other vendors."

"I'm sure," Janet said, nodding.

"We'd have to put you through the gauntlet," Jennifer picked up again. "But it'd be so much fun if we could work together."

"I'd love that!" Janet exclaimed. "I'm sure our team is up to the challenge, no matter what it could end up entailing. Can you imagine what my dad will say if he hears two of his favorite protégés might be working together on the same project?"

Jennifer laughed. "He would definitely be proud."

"I bet he'd be jealous he's not involved."

They both laughed at that, and as they finished their drinks, they talked about old times and memories. Janet found herself really happy at their chance meeting.

As they left Perks, Jennifer said, "Thanks again for the coffee. I really enjoyed catching up. I'll do some asking around and check with my VP on the possibilities for Arachnid. Stay in touch, because I'd hate for this idea to become just a cloud of smoke."

"Hey, I'll see you at Pilates, right?" Janet said. She waved good-bye as Jennifer slipped into her car. "Have a great day!"

THE CAFFEINE KICK WAS RUNNING HIGH WHEN JANET ARRIVED AT ARACH-nid. She strutted past the front desk, tossing out a hearty "Good morning, Sarah!" Down the hallway, Rolland stood outside his of-fice, chatting with Enrique. Nearer, she saw Marcus, and she called out to him as she approached. "Hi, Marcus!" He glanced up and raised a coy hand, then returned to his business.

"Ready, Rolland?" she asked when she reached where he and Enrique stood.

"Yep, all set."

"Did you make it to Pilates this morning?" Enrique asked her.

"Wouldn't miss it," she said. "Still waiting for you to show up one of these days."

Enrique laughed at the remark. "Well, don't get your hopes up," he said. "I don't know where you get the energy. All right, I know you two have a meeting. Don't go too easy on her, Rolland."

ROLLAND STARTED WITH SMALL TALK, ASKING JANET ABOUT HER WEEKEND, inquiring about what, exactly, Pilates entailed and remarking on her cheerful mood. He then moved seamlessly to the heart of their planned discussion.

"You should have gotten a chance to review your activity report," he said. "What trends stood out to you?"

"I did look it over," Janet confirmed, clasping her hands on her lap. "I was excited when I saw just how many Discovery meetings I've completed. I want to keep up that pace."

"I saw that, too," Rolland said. "The count is ahead of schedule. If you're comfortable maintaining that rate, you'll hit your goals in no time."

"I can do that," Janet said.

Rolland pivoted to the next point. "While you're holding more Discovery meetings than you expected, are you seeing the results you'd hoped to from them?"

Janet shifted her weight in the chair. "I'm seeing more suc-cess," she said. "At the same time, I guess I would have hoped more closed deals would result from all the extra meetings."

"I hear you," Rolland said. "What do you suppose might be hindering your progress?"

"It seems like the deals are always going great and the prospects are open and share their needs with me," Janet said. Her words then took on a frustrated tone. "But when it comes time to work on solutions together, some of them stop following up with me and returning my calls. Once, a client told me they just weren't ready to move forward at that time. But I checked back in with them a few weeks later to see where they were at, and I found out they'd gone ahead with another vendor!"

Rolland grimaced in an *I've-been-there* way. "That's a frustrating situation," he said. "It makes sense to me that you're somebody your prospects really like and enjoy getting to know. You're engaging and have high energy."

"I know!" Janet said. "That's what I try to bring to it."

"At the same time," Rolland continued, "I wonder: do you think it's possible those same traits are being viewed as youth and inexperience? Do you think maybe your lack of technical background doesn't leave them with the confidence in the solutions you're bringing?"

Janet's brow furrowed. "You know, I see what you're saying," she conceded. "I guess I'd never thought of it that way. Do people really think like that?"

"Unfortunately, they might." Rolland offered a sympathetic smile, then went on. "I'm curious: have you been taking a sales engineer along with you at those points?"

"Sure, sometimes. I've brought Marcus along on a few." Janet then described the opportunities that she and Marcus had worked on together.

"OK," Rolland said. "It sounds like you're heading in the right direction. But a couple of those deals sound like they have more to do with desktop and software applications, which Sharon would be better suited for. Marcus specializes more in hardware and networking implementation."

Janet cringed. "I don't know, Rolland. Sharon is a tough personality sometimes. I wouldn't exactly say she's a people person. Do you really think that having Sharon along would help in a sales situation?"

"I understand your question, and I can't say you're wrong about Sharon's personality," Rolland acknowledged. "However, clients aren't expecting sales engineers to have great social skills. They're expecting the engineer to simply be an expert. The expertise the engineer shares gives them confidence that the solution will work."

"I know," Janet said. "Marcus does a great job of demonstrating his expertise. And we have great chemistry; we work together really well."

Rolland frowned. "Let's try taking this case by case, Janet. You're doing a great job lately, so we just want to make sure we're doing what we can to propel you even further."

"I appreciate that," she said. "I'll really try to think through who would be best to bring into these meetings."

"Sure," Rolland said. "Sometimes, that could even mean Enrique or I go with you instead of a sales engineer. Do you think perhaps that could mitigate any wrong perceptions of inexperience that prospects might be holding against you?" Janet nodded, and Rolland went on. "That would also give us a chance to talk about what we observe together."

Janet nodded again. "I get what you're saying, Rolland. And as long as we're looking ahead, I do have one thing to share with you. I know it's not exactly Activity Review material, but I wanted to bring it up while we were one-on-one."

Rolland held up a hand. "I'm eager to hear it, but let's wrap up this portion of the meeting first. So what adjustments are you open to making going forward?"

"Sure," Janet said. "I'll give what you said a shot and mix up the group from time to time. I'll look to involve Enrique in on some deals. And even Sharon if the situation calls for it."

"Excellent," Rolland said. "I'm looking forward to seeing what impact that has on helping you move deals through your funnel. Now, tell me about this other thing."

A renewed wave of excitement from the coffee shop meeting rolled over Janet. "I met up with a friend this morning—Jennifer—who has a new job over at Hallmark," she said. "She's spearheading this grand initiative over there and wants to explore the possibility of using us as a technology and networking partner." She went on, excitedly explaining to Rolland all of the aspects Jennifer had shared. Janet followed by sharing her own thoughts about where Arachnid could fit in.

"Hallmark, huh?" Rolland didn't need to say it: Hallmark would be a massive account if Arachnid could land it. "I'd like to stay close to this opportunity. As you go further, make sure you keep the CRM records up-to-date. After you've done a bit more Discovery, would you like to work together on some strategy?"

"Yes, I think that'd be helpful," Janet said. "I'll schedule a Pre-Call Meeting with you."

"Great. Well done, Janet. Way to get your foot in the door. That is an exciting opportunity!"

After the meeting ended, Janet immediately texted Jennifer to share her work information and calendar openings. Janet was encouraged hearing Rolland's optimism about the deal. She didn't want to waste any time.

A FEW WEEKS LATER, AFTER MORE DISCOVERY CALLS WITH JENNIFER AND even an onsite visit at Hallmark to get a feel for their operations, Janet took a call she'd been hoping for at work.

"I've been talking up Arachnid to my VP, Robert," Jennifer told her. "He's very interested to hear what Arachnid has to offer in terms of general capabilities and also specifically on your network support system expertise. I didn't realize this before, but he indicated to me privately that a current preferred vendor has had a few missteps recently. Although we're still doing business with them, Robert was actually wanting to explore what other teams might be able to bring to the table. He's heard positive things about Arachnid, and my confidence in you and your team was even more reassuring."

"This is wonderful," Janet said. "What can we do?"

"He encouraged me to see about having you do a presentation at the IT Directors meeting," Jennifer said. Her voice now lowered. "Now, Janet, listen closely. I don't know if you realize how big of an opportunity this is. From what I understand, companies try for years to get a chance to present to this group and potentially be brought in as a preferred vendor. Your timing on this is incredible, and I can't tell you how excited I am for you. I'll do whatever I can to support you and help you in preparing. This could be even bigger down the road than just working with me."

"Excellent!" Janet said. "Thank you, Jenny. I'll let my team know so that we can get our heads together on the presentation. When do you want to see us?"

"Well, actually, there is a meeting coming up in two weeks if you thought your team would be ready. Otherwise we'd have to wait until the next Directors meeting, which would be in three months. But, that's not the end of the world because we wouldn't be too far down the road next quarter on my projects."

"Oh, no, we'll be there," Janet said. "Put us down for the presentation in two weeks and we'll make it happen. Thanks so much, Jenny."

After the call ended, Janet's thoughts strung out in excitement. *Yes! We're in now! I can't wait to tell Rolland—we need to Pre-call.* As she contemplated how large of a client Hallmark would be, she had a further thought: *I need Enrique to come with me. Hallmark could make my career!* And then: *I'm so overwhelmed that Jenny is making this happen. Her name is on the line for us, and I've got to make her proud.*

Janet got up from her desk and quickly made her way to Rolland's office. She burst through the door without a knock and announced, "It's happening, Rolland! Hallmark wants us to present."

Rolland looked up. "Phenomenal news, Janet, way to go!" He looked back across his desk to where Brad was sitting; the two of them had been in the middle of a One-on-One Debrief. "Hey, Brad, this sounds exciting, doesn't it?" Rolland turned back to Janet. "Thanks for sharing, Janet. Let me and Brad finish up. Do you think you'd want to put some ideas together and maybe touch base tomorrow morning to discuss this? I think Monroe is going to be in then, too, so we could pull him in on it, too."

"I'll get on it," Janet said. She looked at Brad. "Brad, I'm so sorry for interrupting. I just got so excited." Turning back toward Rolland, she went on. "Tomorrow morning sounds great, see you then."

Once back at her desk, Janet began putting together her Precall Plan. She pulled up all of her notes to help her summarize the deal's background information. *Arachnid is already positioned well in Robert's mind, thanks to Jenny,* she thought. *I can start the presentation introducing our general capabilities; that's easy enough.*

As she moved into thinking about specific network capabilities, Janet wondered if Enrique would be willing to give a case study on how Arachnid had supported larger customers. *If we're going to convince Hallmark we should be on the preferred vendor's list,* she thought, *then bringing a big hitter like Enrique along will pay dividends.* After drafting her plan, Janet emailed it to Rolland.

THE NEXT DAY, JANET COULD SCARCELY CONCENTRATE DURING HER EAR-ly-morning Pilates class. In a way, she was relieved to see that Jennifer wasn't there. It wasn't that Janet didn't want to see her or was ungrateful for the opportunity—far from it. But she also wanted a respite, however brief, from the consuming thoughts of the opportunity with Hallmark. She knew how big it could be, for Arachnid and for her. Rolland had her Pre-call Plan in hand and would be reviewing it with her when she got to work. She was excited for that. A little nervous, too. *The good kind of nervous,* she told herself.

At Arachnid, she gathered with Rolland and Monroe in Rolland's office.

"I read your email," Rolland told her. "Solid work so far, Janet. I can tell you've been striving to improve the quality of your meetings. I feel like I've been a part of this deal just by reading over your notes. It seems that you think we're at the Presentation stage." Janet nodded enthusiastically. "I agree with you," Rolland went on. "In reviewing the plan specifically, it sounds like you want to take Enrique along."

"I do."

"I think that's a great idea," he said.

Janet detailed her thought process. "I did think about making the presentation a Four-Legged Call and maybe even opening the team up to include you as well, Rolland," she said. "I would open the meeting and give the presentation on general capabilities, and then Enrique could share how we've done networking strategies for other large clients like Sprint—sort of as a testimonial and proof of concept."

"Glad to hear that," he replied. "And I agree with you. As part of this plan, then, it will be important to clearly define what each of your roles will be, so you'll need to coordinate together on that. I know last time we talked about sales engineers, we discussed not taking Marcus so often. However, in this instance the project would actually be perfectly in his wheelhouse, so you might even want to consider involving him instead of me. He'll fulfill a more unique role as opposed to bringing me when you already have Enrique there as the senior sales-team member."

"That's great," she said.

Monroe jumped in. "Think of it like running a basketball offense. You need to know who has the ball at any given time and when it's appropriate to pass it around."

"That makes sense," Janet said. "I'll give some thought to what roles we should each play."

"On a separate note," Monroe said, "of the potential objections that could possibly surface, what is the most likely issue that has the ability to derail the A-plan, and what is your backup strategy to address it?"

The question snagged Janet. She took a breath. "I have to admit, I haven't given much thought to backup plans," she said.

"That's all right. It's important to be optimistic and go into a meeting with the expectation that your plan is going to work." Monroe said. "At the same time, there could always be a curveball. For instance, you're pretty confident the presentation is going to be about general capabilities, but what if you get in there and one of the IT directors asks for a specific strategy for implementation of one of Jennifer's first rollout objectives and wants a ballpark estimate?"

Janet shuddered as she imagined that scenario. "Yikes," she said.

"See what I mean?" Monroe said, nodding.

"I wouldn't be ready for that at all, at this point," Janet conceded. "I guess we could have Marcus put together some numbers on that and have those in our back pocket so I could then provide ranges of prices. But it seems like it wouldn't be good to try giving them a specific quote at that time. What do you think?"

"That's good," Monroe said. "You don't want to be quoting on a backup plan without having ensured you understand all of the BANTC and specifically that director's potential perspective on the quote. Remember: a firm quote on paper should be nothing more than documentation of what's already been agreed to in principle."

"You're right," Janet said. "So I could give the range, but then indicate that our process is to give accurate quotes based on complete information. We'd be happy to go in, do some analysis, and determine a best-fit solution first in order to provide a quote we are confident in."

Monroe tapped the table twice with his pen. "Very good. I gave you an example of a trigger that would cause you to go to that B-plan. Are there any other things that would trigger you to say that we ought to share some price ranges on a particular project or ask for an opportunity to send in engineers to do an analysis?"

Janet considered the question, impressed that Monroe was

putting her through these anticipatory paces. "If we hear the directors asking questions that pertain more to us performing immediate services instead of just being added to the preferred vendor's list, then that might be a trigger as well," she said.

Rolland and Janet then went back and forth a while longer on her various strategies and how they anticipated the directors would respond at each point in the meeting. Rolland said, "Let's quickly look at the opening of your agenda together. When you're giving a presentation, it's important to give some background first. It may seem like you're telling the directors things they already know, but at the same time you're actually demonstrating your understanding of their needs. It also lets you set the stage for why what you're about to present is relevant to them."

They went on discussing the significance of making sure everyone in the room would emotionally buy in to each aspect of the presentation. The aim, at the end, would be to set up an easy "yes" from the prospective client. Before wrapping up the meeting, Rolland asked, "Do you have any other questions for me, Janet?"

"Nope, I'm all set," she said. "It seems like we have the right people and all the right tools. This is going to be a home run of a presentation."

JANET STOOD BEFORE HER FULL-LENGTH MIRROR ON SATURDAY NIGHT, taking in what she saw. She'd been waiting for this all week, as her nervous energy about the Hallmark presentation steadily built. Date night would be the perfect antidote to that pressure, a chance to spend some casual time with a guy she'd found herself getting close to. By chance, he'd recommended Airborne!, the new trampoline park in town. That would be the perfect venue for blowing off some steam, she figured.

When the knock on the door came, Janet smiled at her reflection. "He's here," she said. She turned, and strode eagerly for the door, throwing it open.

"Hi, Marcus!"

He put a hand over his heart and took a step back, grinning widely. "Wow, Janet, lookin' spicy," he said. "I thought we were just going to the trampoline park. You look like you're ready for a night on the town."

Janet grabbed his hand and pulled him inside. "Don't be silly," she said, reveling at the compliment nonetheless. "This is just my normal weekend attire. You don't think I'm overdressed, do you?"

"No, not at all." He kissed her on the cheek. "You look great. Let's go."

WHILE MARCUS DROVE, JANET LOOKED AT THE AIRBORNE! WEBSITE ON HER smartphone. "Obstacle courses, dodgeball, foam pits," she said. "This is exactly what I need."

"It's going to be a blast," Marcus said.

"I may even show you some of my gymnastics skills from my cheerleading days," Janet said with a wink. "If I have any left."

"Can't wait."

Janet laced her hand in his. Marcus glanced at her and smiled.

"I'm really glad you're going to be at the presentation Tuesday," she said. "It gives me confidence."

"Good. I'm excited to be there."

After a brief lull in the conversation, Janet said, "I had a slightly odd conversation with Rolland during my last Activity Review."

"Oh?" Marcus looked at her again. "What about?"

"About you and me spending too much time together."

Marcus sputtered. "Wait, what? First of all, that's none of his business. Second…"

"I misspoke," Janet said. "It wasn't about you and me dating. He was concerned that we work on too many of my sales together. He thinks some of the deals fell more in Sharon's"—she put a mocking emphasis on the name—"wheelhouse and that I ought to involve *her*."

Janet rolled her eyes and sighed. "Sharon," she said again in that dismissive way. "Like she's supposed to help me get deals."

Marcus squeezed her hand. "He's not wrong, you know." When Janet bristled, he spoke more softly. "Some of the deals we've gone out on probably should have had her."

"Sharon really rubs some people the wrong way," Janet protested. "I like working on projects with you. You know technology *and* you're a nice person. Don't you like doing deals together?"

Marcus reached out and rested his right hand on Janet's shoulder. "Of course I like working together. At the same, for everything that Sharon isn't, she's also extremely good at what she does. I want to see you succeed as much as possible, so if that means sometimes you work with Sharon, I say give it a shot."

Janet sighed. "I suppose you're right. I'll give this one to you and

Rolland. But, you better make it up to me by doing the obstacle course tonight. No chickening out!"

THE FIRST HOUR AT THE TRAMPOLINE PARK FLEW BY, AS JANET AND MARCUS bounced around and laughed. In the dodgeball area, Marcus talked Janet into a second game and then a third; evading flying projectiles was more his speed. At last, she pulled away, urging him to the obstacle course, her favored area.

"Let's wait a bit," Marcus said. "The line is pretty long over there."

Janet looked toward the line and smirked. "What are you talking about? There's, like, five people. Come on, we're going." She hooked her arm in his and began pulling him toward the course.

After a short wait, their turn came up. When the whistle blew, Janet was quick out of the blocks, springing up to the first platform. She made it to the end of the rope swing well ahead of Marcus, who'd slipped and tumbled into the foam pit below. As he tried to fight his way back onto the course, Janet whimsically bounced onward, putting significant distance between them.

She gave a backward glance as she reached the final obstacle, a fire pole that she had to descend to reach the finish line.

"Bye, bye, Marcus," she shouted with a smile and a wave. "See you at the finish, if you ever get there." She seized the fire pole with both hands and launched herself.

Suddenly, one of her hands came free from the pole, and Janet tumbled awkwardly to the bottom, landing hard on her feet. The right ankle twisted on impact, and constellations of pain shot up through her leg.

"Owwwwwwww!" she wailed. Behind her, compelled by her scream, Marcus picked up the pace, reaching the fire pole and flying down to be with her. Janet was now in a seated position, holding her stricken ankle with both hands.

"Don't stand up," he said. "Let me look."

He gingerly took hold of her leg. She released her hands. What they saw shocked both of them. The ankle was already ballooning, nearly the size of a softball.

"Oh, no," she said.

"Stay off that leg," he said, standing up. "Let me help." He dipped his shoulders and got his arms underneath Janet's, then helped her to a one-legged standing position. He then swept her into his arms and carried her toward the car.

"Emergency room?" Janet said, her voice trembling.

"I think so. We have to get it looked at, at least."

As Marcus drove, Janet grew increasingly frantic about the injury. "This is such bad timing," she said. "What's going to happen with the meeting?"

"It's going to be fine," Marcus said.

"I need to text Jennifer. She needs to know."

"Now?"

"Yes," Janet said. "Now."

She punched the message into her phone: *Jenny, I'm not sure if I'll be able to attend the presentation or not. I think I broke my foot and I don't know when/if I'll need surgery.*

"Can you call Enrique?" she asked Marcus. "He should know sooner rather than later. He may have to do this presentation."

"Now?" Marcus asked, frowning. "I mean, I'm sure we'll be fine either way. Besides, it's late."

"Please, Marcus. Just call him."

"Once we're at the hospital, I will."

J ANET RECEIVED PAIN MEDICATION AND A PLACE TO SIT IN THE EXAM ROOM until she could be taken back for an MRI. She and Marcus sat quietly, each in thought, until she nudged him and asked, "Have you called him yet?"

"Who?"

"Enrique. Your uncle. You know who."

They'd spoken of the family dynamic when they started seeing each other, and they'd agreed to be circumspect. Neither had figured on breaking the news of their dating this way.

Marcus sighed. "OK, fine. I'll call him." He patted her knee, then stood and left the room, finding a quiet corner in the hallway to make the call. After several rings, and just as Marcus considered hanging up, a groggy voice came on the line.

"Uncle Enrique?"

"Who is this?"

"Marcus."

"What time is it?"

Marcus looked at his watch. "A little after eleven."

Alertness came into Enrique's voice. "Marcus? Everything OK?"

"Well, I'm OK," Marcus said. "I'm down at the ER."

"ER? What? Why?"

"It's OK," Marcus said, soothingly. "I'm here with Janet."

"Janet? What the—"

"It looks like she might have broken her ankle at the trampoline park, and she needed a ride to the ER, and—"

"Wait a minute. She called you from the trampoline park?"

"Well, no."

"Well, what?"

Marcus paced down the hallway. "We were there together."

The door to the exam room came open, and Janet hopped on one foot into the hallway. Marcus dropped the phone from his ear. "Janet, what are you—"

"Tell him we can't reschedule." She hopped closer. "Tell him he'll have to do the presentation without me if I can't make it." From the phone came static squawking from Enrique. Marcus put it to his ear again.

"Did you hear that?" Marcus asked.

"I think I get what's going on," Enrique said. "Just make sure she's taken care of, OK?"

"OK."

"Tell her not to worry about Tuesday."

"I'll tell her."

"I think I get the picture here," Enrique said. "I don't need to hear any more about the two of you. But Marcus…"

"Yes, Uncle Enrique?"

"I'll see *you* at family dinner tomorrow. Understand?"

"I understand."

ON THE DAY OF THE PRESENTATION, THE ARACHNID TEAM STOOD IN THE Hallmark lobby and waited for Jennifer and her VP, Robert, to come down and greet them. Enrique, the veteran of so many deals, stood calmly, taking in the details of the place. Next to him was Marcus, fidgety and anxious but also ready. And, finally, on crutches, there was Janet, broken ankle and all. She wouldn't have missed it for anything.

Jennifer smiled wide when she saw them, especially Janet, whose terse text had left her wondering who would show up today.

"Welcome to Hallmark, everyone," Jennifer said, as introductions were made.

Jennifer and Robert led the group to the meeting room where the IT Directors had gathered. Janet was then given the floor.

First, she reviewed the agenda, just as she'd planned with Monroe. The Hallmark team was in agreement with the plan, so Janet pivoted to what she had learned about Hallmark and its needs from Jennifer, as well as the potential projects that lay ahead.

"I'd like to introduce Enrique Dumas, our senior salesperson," Janet now said. "He can give you some background on our experience with large companies like yours and the support you can expect from us." Enrique then took command of the meeting. He was equal parts informative, authoritative, and charming.

When the directors' questions took a turn toward technical aspects, Janet introduced Marcus, who delivered detailed answers that seemed to meet with approval. At every turn of the meeting, an Arachnid team member was able to step up and deliver what the client needed and wanted to hear.

It's incredible to work alongside such an impressive team, Janet thought as she listened to Marcus.

When the presentation wound down, Janet stepped in again to wrap things up. "We hope we've provided what you need to understand about us," she said. "We would greatly appreciate the opportunity to join Hallmark's preferred-vendors list. I know this is our presentation, but I'd like to ask: What do you all see as the next steps we should take together in this evaluation?"

The VP, Robert, said, "Thank you for your time today." He looked at the directors in a way that suggested he had the group's tacit permission to answer. "I'll chat with you about that as I see you to the lobby." After a round of handshakes, Robert led the Arachnid team out.

"It was a strong presentation," he told them. "The directors and I will be meeting to consider this opportunity. I'm sure we'll have information to pass along within the next week."

Enrique, Janet, and Marcus rode back to the office together, Marcus at the wheel. Enrique turned in his seat and looked at Janet. "That was impressive," he said. "You have a lot of talent. I used to think Rolland and I were the dynamic duo, but it sure looks like you can fill these shoes before long. Which is good, because somebody has to pick up the slack when I move on." He grinned at her.

"Thank you, Enrique," Janet said.

He gave her a wink. "There should always be a strong salesperson in the family."

Janet blushed. Marcus chuckled. "All right, all right," he said.

Janet looked out the window at the homes and businesses streaming by. She thought of the failed sales call with Rolland not so long ago, and the fear and self-doubt that had come of that. She thought of the new focus on measuring activity and really bearing down to identify the deals with the best potential. She thought of Hawaii. And she smiled widely, her optimism about all things in full bloom.

And as joyful as she was in that moment, it didn't compare with the excitement that came just a day later, as Janet listened to the voicemail from Jennifer:

"Congratulations! I just heard that it's official. Robert and the directors want to provisionally add Arachnid to our preferred vendors list. We'd like to have your team come do a systems analysis, and put together a proposal and a quote as soon as possible. Based on the outcomes of that, we should be able to solidify Arachnid's position."

THE FOLLOWING MONDAY CAME, AND DOM SUMMONED ROLLAND AND Monroe to his office in advance of the sales-team meeting. Dom had pulled the forecast report from the CRM system so they all had the updated numbers.

"We've had a notably strong quarter," Dom said. "That's great to see. Congratulations, Rolland."

Rolland looked over the numbers on the sheet. "I'm more than pleased," he said. "Everyone on the team is improving. Janet's Hallmark deal, with Enrique, is as good as closed. Enrique has upsold some of his existing clients and has already brought in some larger projects. Diane's off and running. Even Brad has turned the corner. We're seeing some singles and doubles out of him."

"It all shows," Dom said. "But I'm even more pleased with the bigger goals we've accomplished this year. Back when Monroe first came in, we had major targets in place. Not only were we looking to expand, but we wanted to hire a new salesperson and we had some serious evaluating to do with Brad as well. Clearly, hiring Diane was the right choice, and that relieved a bit of stress from your plate, Rolland. Where would you say we stand now with Brad?"

"It's taken a long time to get him to where he is," Rolland said. "If you'd asked me six months ago, I wouldn't have thought he could be where he is now. He's still a teacher at heart, and he still likes to do more presenting than I'd prefer, but he's coming around. He's focusing on the meetings we're having together. More important, *he* recognizes the changes he needs to make and he's actively working with me to get there. What would you say, Monroe?"

"Bottom line?" Monroe said. "He's shown enough growth and self-determination that he's worth Rolland's efforts to continue working with him. I think with the progress he's made, we should give him another quarter. My guess is he'll be on track by the end of that quarter."

Dom smiled. "I don't take letting someone go lightly, so based upon what both of you have said, it sounds like he's on the right trajectory and worth investing in. I'm also happy we have the results to allow us to make that investment now. Also, what makes me happier than even the closed sales is the size and quality of the pipeline you guys have built."

"Absolutely, Dom," Rolland said. "In the past, the funnel and forecast were made up of whatever people happened to put in, and the way I dealt with it was figuring half of it was complete junk; I just didn't know which half. Now I believe very strongly that eighty percent of the deals that are in the forecastable part of the funnel will come to fruition. And, the rest of the funnel represents enough opportunities that it will continue to be full. That Funnel Review that Monroe taught me how to do has really changed the game."

"I've noticed that confidence in you develop as well," Monroe added. "You've really grasped all of the processes we've practiced. Now you've got a repeatable method in place to follow, and it should continue providing you with those predictable results you're talking about."

Rolland appreciated the praise and validation. "Absolutely," he said. "I'm in more control of the destiny of our sales team. I feel like my efforts are actually being spent in the right places and bringing about appropriate growth in each of the team members. Had you asked me last year to increase sales by twenty percent I wouldn't have known what to do, and I would've been crossing all my fingers and toes in hopes of pulling it off. Today, I'm very confident I would be able to hit the right buttons within the team to drive in the direction we need as a company."

The three of them wrapped up the meeting and headed down the hall to the conference room, where the rest of the sales team was congregated with their coffee and donuts. The mood was light and positive. Everyone shared a sense of camaraderie and optimism. Rolland got their attention, began the meeting in its usual fashion, and eventually introduced Dom for a big announcement.

"I'll get right to it," Dom told them. "We just got done looking over the most recent forecast report, and I've got to say: You all have been at the top of your game. I'd also like to share that I've got a ribbon-cutting scheduled in Springfield! A team has been hired, the offices have been set up, and none of that would have been possible without the hard work all of you have put in this year. This is your win."

A round of applause greeted Dom's announcement, and he encouraged the cheers, then asked for quiet again to finish up.

"I'm proud of each of you for the strides you've made and to Rolland for the changes he's been willing to implement and push forward." Dom now pointed to Monroe. "I'd also like to thank Monroe for his part in our growth. And don't worry, we're not letting him off the hook just yet. He'll be joining the team down in Springfield to make sure they get off on the right foot and function consistently with the practices that we've instituted here."

Takeaways

A Really Big Deal

Meeting Cadence, Activity Review, Pre-Call Plan, and the 4-Legged Sales Call

W HEN WE FIRST MET ROLLAND, HE WAS FACING SEVERAL CHALLENGES. Brad wasn't producing and Rolland thought he needed to be replaced. At the same time, he already had a vacancy on the team and wasn't prepared to create another. He also was training Janet, whose inexperience showed as she bulldozed a presentation. Rolland was even questioning whether being a manager was a role he wanted to continue with. He was prepared to hand Dom his resignation and go back to simply selling.

I've spoken with many sales managers who empathize with Rolland. They've said, "I feel like my success depends on a roll of the dice. I try to pretend that I'm steering the ship, but when I get home I realize there wasn't much during the day I was able to be proactive about."

Rolland admitted as much at the end of this chapter when he said, "Had you asked me last year to increase sales by twenty percent I wouldn't have known what to do, and I would've been crossing all my fingers and toes in hopes of pulling it off."

What he needed was a new approach. What he needed was to retake control of not only his sales team, but their results. Rolland used to view management as putting out fires, and driving people by asking for more, and telling them they hadn't produced enough. As we reflect on his journey with Monroe, however, we can see how he has adopted a system of intentional actions and refocused his time and energy on optimizing the results of his team.

Before he started working with Monroe, Rolland would've sworn he couldn't take on any extra meetings. He felt he was running at full speed as it was. However, while working with Monroe, he instituted a handful of new, regularly scheduled meetings with his team members. Some happen frequently such as the Weekly Sales Team Meeting. Others are more spread out, like the Activity Review, and some are even scheduled on a case-by-case basis, such as the Pre-Call Planning meetings. Since Janet participated in those specific meetings, we'll dig into the agendas and goals of her meetings with Rolland shortly.

> Maintain focus by redirecting urgent "Got a minute?" requests into a schedule of short, productive meetings.

Most of the managers I know have been reluctant to add meetings to their schedule and their salespeople's schedules. In fact, they've even echoed their salespeople by saying, "Every moment in the office is a moment wasted not selling." However, the reason that their meetings aren't seen as productive is not because meetings in general are bad, but because the meetings they've been *having* are bad. The meetings didn't consistently add value for the salesperson each and every time. Sales managers also tend to handle important topics whenever they arise. Sales people will drop in asking, "Got a minute?" So by the time a meeting rolls around, most of the important matters have already been addressed and topics left for the meeting are of little value. A better practice is to maintain focus for yourself and your team by redirecting each non-urgent "Got a minute?" into a well-understood schedule of short, productive meetings.

Rolland recognized that the "Got a minute" distractions weren't going to work as demonstrated by his reaction when Janet came bursting in to announce she'd landed the presentation with Hallmark. Rolland wasn't rude or dismissive, but he did remind her that they would catch up and handle that topic in a meeting the next day. Rather than interrupt his One-on-One Debrief with Brad and then try to get back on track, Rolland had learned how to organize his meetings efficiently, and does so now with more structure and a set agenda. So, even when Janet had exciting news to share in her meeting with him, Rolland told her, "Before we get into that, let's finish our Activity Review."

These practices ensure that the scheduled meetings aren't wasting anyone's time and that you can be more efficient by not dealing with interruptions. Since managing people can hardly be done without having face-to-face conversations, meetings are the bedrock of your management efforts. The key is to structure the agendas and participants of each meeting efficiently to generate the most productivity for team members. So, let's take look at a simple meeting structure, around which most of the functions of management can be fulfilled.

The agendas and scheduling of the new meetings Rolland instituted were always structured. They had a specific, predictable cadence, which is valuable for everyone. The sales team knew when to expect a debrief meeting as opposed to a mentoring session. Rolland could be sure his time was most efficiently spent by focusing only on the set agenda for any current meeting because he knew that other matters would be addressed at a later time.

Mapping out your meetings consistently also allows you to balance the management themes of each. Recall in the Team Balloon Model that Accountability and Support walls were used to put pressure on the balloons and lift the revenue bar. The ISM system organizes most managerial responsibilities into eight meetings that apply pressure to one of the balloon walls at regular intervals.

Throughout Rolland's journey, we've seen him incorporate several Support meetings such as the **Pre-Call Plan**, the **Post-Call Debrief**, and the **Sales Focus Blueprint Meeting**. The other meetings intended for Support are the **One-on-One Mentoring Meeting**, which Monroe actually conducted with Rolland as the person being mentored and the weekly **Sales Team Meeting**. In the last chapter we touched on how the Sales Team Meeting, along with properly designed contests and compensation, is used to provide motivation; and Rolland has continued developing his agenda for it to meet that goal. Then in this chapter we saw Janet in an **Activity Review Meeting**, Brad interrupted in a **One-on-One Debrief** Meeting, and Rolland observing the **Funnel Review** meeting's impact on the forecast. These meetings are all Accountability-based.

While we did not observe complete execution of each Accountability meeting, it is important to recognize the importance that the Accountability Wall has in the Team Balloon Model. It is especially important to gaining predictability and control of sales results. An overview of those remaining meetings will be shared in the Epilogue.

Maintaining a fair balance between these different meetings protects a manager from appearing too much like a drill sergeant on one end or like a cheerleader on the other. The balance also ensures that each salesperson is receiving equal portions of the ingredients necessary to grow and succeed. Although Accountability-based meetings aren't often eagerly anticipated, they do refine a salesperson's focus. Janet told Jennifer that she was originally skeptical of attending meetings like the Activity Review, but after going through them, she recognized how they helped her improve her selling process.

Activity Review Meetings

A N Activity Review meeting is an opportunity to take the pulse of an existing Sales Focus Blueprint to make sure it's still working efficiently. The best plans are only as good as their execution. While plans should be stuck to, they should also be fluid enough to respond to new information.

Football coaches have well-designed game plans based on the best available intel and stats. If the football team's strongest asset is its running game, then the game plan will rely heavily on it. However, if the opposing defense puts pressure on the running game, then the coach needs to call a few passing plays to keep the team moving forward. Or, perhaps if the opponent gets an early lead, then in an effort to manage the clock, the coach could also lean on the passing game. No matter the scenario, the game plan must adapt to new circumstances to maximize success.

Similarly, once you've scheduled an Activity Review, prepare for it by gathering available data to spot trends ahead of time. With a CRM, pulling a report will be easier, but logbooks and calendars can also provide what you need. Consider how that information relates to the plan the salesperson intended to put in motion after the Sales Focus Blueprint Meeting. Trends can be telling. Trends can also be adjusted.

Activity Reviews lift salespeople to see the bird's-eye view of their territory rather than the specifics of each deal.

It's not realistic to dig into every possible activity of a salesperson. And most salespeople don't respond well to being micromanaged. So, the Activity Review should bring the salesperson up to take a bird's-eye view of their forest (or territory) as a whole rather than zeroing in on a couple specific trees (or deals).

If there are outlying trends impacting a salesperson's overall success, then those are "the what" you want to discuss during the meeting. Several trends could be manifesting, and each warrants a unique modification to the ongoing plan.

The key trends to be mindful of are:

» **Overall Effort Level** – Is the salesperson working in alignment with prior commitments and expectations?

» **Effort Level by Type of Activity** – Is the salesperson focusing their energy across all activities, or are they giving preference to some activities over others?

» **Effort Level by Revenue Stream** – Has the salesperson found significant success in a single stream and therefore put off efforts in other areas of their plan?

» **Success Ratios Between Activity Types and Revenue Streams** – Is the salesperson experiencing higher or lower conversion ratios than expected that need to be adjusted accordingly?

» **Timing** – Is the salesperson balancing their time and efforts between the top and bottom of the sales funnel as appropriate?

You'll want to ask yourself these questions in preparation because they will become the agenda for the actual Activity Review. When you're looking at the statistics, if you start to notice that results aren't measuring up to the salesperson's goals, then you'll want to plan to discuss what factors are causing the poor performance.

At the beginning of the meeting, present the information you have to the salesperson and ask them what they see. With Janet, Rolland asked, "What trends stood out to you?" Service Balloon salespeople should be able to lead this discussion on their own without much more prompting, so managers should refrain from submitting more than perhaps a single "by the way" sort of comment.

However, Rolland continued to coach Janet, a Partner Balloon salesperson, by asking follow-up questions. As much as an Activity Review is about Accountability, it can also be spun into a coaching opportunity. Janet recognized that she was hitting her activity targets, but she wasn't generating proportionate success in her sales. Once they spotted the trend together, Rolland dug deeper for details that could help explain the gap.

The tenure, or Balloon level, of the salesperson will influence whether they should come up with their own adjustments or if the manager should suggest them. Rolland and Janet brainstormed the idea of bringing others along during the Collaboration stage of deals and, more so, to base who she brings according to the specific opportunity. Unfortunately salespeople, especially ones in the Assess Balloon, sometimes fail to meet their activity targets. Had that been the case for Janet, Rolland would've reminded her where the activity-expectations bar was and asked her what she planned to change to get back on track.

As you review current circumstances with the salesperson, you should discuss whether they are still comfortable that they will reach their goals based on where they currently stand or if they need to modify the plan to better align with their actual experience.

> Too often, salespeople believe they can reduce their activities and still obtain the same results.

If they choose to modify the plan, ensure all the implications of the change are enumerated because the final results are likely to change. Too often, salespeople believe they can reduce their activities and still obtain the same results. At this point, recap and validate the salesperson's commitment to all the proposed changes for their activity plan. A best practice is to have the salesperson email you with their new commitments. This ensures they have a clear understanding of the goals and won't be confused when the next review comes.

In Rolland and Janet's meeting, she wanted to talk about her meeting with Jennifer before the Activity Review agenda was finished. This is common; salespeople really like to tell their stories. But a trend is not the result of a specific deal or story. It is based on the overarching habits and averages associated with a salesperson's plan and activities. So, Rolland kept Janet on topic and finished the Activity Review. He needed her to say, for herself, that she agreed to take steps to improve her discovery-to-presentation-closing ratio by involving other people in her deals when appropriate and to take advantage of all the available resources Arachnid had to offer—not just use her favorite sales engineer.

It's important to remember that this meeting isn't designed to address every trend or potential problem at once. There's no guarantee that by the next meeting, the salesperson's bottom line will miraculously improve no matter how thorough your Activity Review is. The goal is to highlight one or two trends that can be incrementally adjusted over time.

All of the Arachnid salespeople had their own game plan to reach personal goals. Brad, Janet and Diane also broke down their individual targets into activities such as holding more Discovery meetings. Even Enrique had set out to increase how often he made contact with his current accounts. These sorts of plans are great starts to improve and develop your team. Unfortunately, too often I've seen that even if a manager proactively developed plans with their salespeople, those plans often get left on the shelf. And, the manager waits until the end of the year to dust them off and analyze the results as if they were still relevant.

The scheduling of Activity Reviews should be based on each salesperson's Balloon Level. With Assess Balloon salespeople it's best to hold these meetings frequently, because they're being measured based on their activity performance and require a greater level of accountability for completion. Remember that with the Assess Balloon, it is the manager's responsibility to set the minimum bar for a salesperson's achievement. If they're becoming successful, frequent review will encourage them to maintain their efforts and allow you to extend them more trust. If they're underperforming, they'll know early enough to correct any actions that are steering them off course.

On the other hand, Activity Reviews should be less frequent for Partner and Service Balloon salespeople because their Sales Plans are more about what they've decided they *want* to accomplish instead of the manager setting the bar. Rolland's understanding with Enrique was that his targets for calling on existing clients were for his own benefit. If Rolland were to take Enrique to task for missing his numbers, the nature of their relationship would change. Instead, Rolland has less frequent meetings with Enrique, where he simply asks Enrique for his perspective on possible trends. This is a passive way of taking the pulse and encouraging the salesperson to stop and reflect on their strategy.

Janet indeed took the adjustments to heart. After she'd landed the presentation with Hallmark, one of her first thoughts was that Enrique would be perfect to bring along. Planning ahead for calls and presentations is a great way for a salesperson to ensure they are following best practices rather than shooting from the hip. When Janet burst into Rolland's office to announce her news, Rolland greeted her with congratulations and then suggested she draft a Pre-Call Plan for them to review the next day.

Pre-Call Plans

MANY SALESPEOPLE ARE WILLING TO GO INTO A MEETING WITHOUT AN AGEN-da and simply lean on their gift of gab to be successful during a call. While their innate skills may be good enough to produce positive results 80 percent of the time, those skills alone may not be enough at crunch time when the deal is on the line. Just because a salesperson possesses a skill in improvisation doesn't mean that it's a best practice. A talented football player might be able to simply show up at a pickup game and lead his team to victory, but that relaxed strategy doesn't get a pro-football team to the postseason.

A Pre-Call Plan is a short meeting (fifteen minutes, but can be longer) that can be conducted as needed before a salesperson goes on a call with a client. They aren't needed for every call. But, it's a good idea to hold them frequently with rookie team members, while reserving them for only the most important sales calls for veteran team members. As a starting point for this meeting, a sales-

> Just because a salesperson possesses a skill in improvisation doesn't mean that it's a best practice.

person should be able to quickly provide an overview of the current status of the client relationship and BANTC, the agenda for their upcoming call, and what the intended result of the call should be. And, the salesperson should be able to spell out the "ABZ Strategies" (A-Plan, B-Plan, etc.) necessary to move the client toward that result. This sets the stage for coaching and collaboration. A template is available for download by accessing this book's Companion Resource website—www.acultureofpredictablesales.com that can help guide you and the salesperson through preparing for and having a Pre-Call Plan meeting. Together you may be able to enhance the plan or add extra corporate resources to its execution.

Janet was comfortable with the details of her current relationship with Hallmark. She understood what the presentation's focus should be and she crafted an agenda accordingly. Janet's plan was to open the presentation with a discussion of general capabilities, and then share specifically about Arachnid's ability to deliver for large clients. Her A-Plan strategy for delivering the second half most effectively was to have Enrique along to share his actual experiences with Sprint and other large accounts. She would handle the breadth of Arachnid's service suite and he would lend credibility to the depth of their networking support abilities. Janet also set the intended *goal*—to get Arachnid added to Hallmark's preferred-vendor list.

As Rolland requested, she wrote all of this into her Pre-Call Plan form and sent it to him before the meeting. This is a valuable practice for two reasons: It allows the salesperson to craft a plan of their own to begin with; and, it allows the manager to get caught up on the background details of a sale in advance so the meeting time can be focused on refining the call strategies. For instance, Janet's summary of BANTC indicated the reason for urgency as well as the high level of authority that would be attending the meeting.

When reviewing the plan, you'll want to ensure the stage of the deal is accurately identified and the strategies in place are suited to that stage. You should look at the proposed agenda, analyze whether it follows a positive "mood meter," and consider whether the right sales tools are being used. It is vital that you are using a well-defined sales process. It should define the requirements for each stage. Although a good sales process will define these, it is common for salespeople to overlook or to consciously ignore some of these best practices. Your review should highlight these issues. Let's break down each of these factors in more detail.

Rolland didn't have to spend time discussing the **stage of the deal** because it was clear from Janet's notes that the call was going to be at the Presentation stage. Had there been gaps in her BANTC or had she been basing progress of the deal on her own rose-colored perceptions, then he would've needed to pull back the reins on her plan. In that case, the agenda would need to be revamped to focus on finalizing the Discovery stage and ensuring that the prospect was as ready and willing to discuss solutions as the salesperson was.

Refining the call strategies is where Monroe chimed in with the idea of ABZ Plan strategies. Most salespeople are able and willing to draft a Primary Call (A-Plan) Strategy, just as Janet was. However, coming up with a Backup plan or even a worst-case-scenario Zero Plan, is not a common practice. Monroe sympathized with Janet when he told her, "It's important to be optimistic and go into a meeting with the expectation that your plan is going to work." At the same time, they would hate to see the upcoming presentation tank over a minor speed bump that could have been anticipated.

That's where B and Z strategies come in. When developing a B-Plan the question to ask is, as Monroe posed, "Of the potential objections that could possibly surface, what is the most likely issue that has the ability to derail the A-Plan?" To develop the B-Plan, sales-team members needed to determine how the presentation could get derailed and identify the trigger that would indicate it. While one B-plan for the primary objection is typically sufficient, sometimes it's reasonable to have multiple B-Plans depending on how likely different objections are to occur. B-Plans are designed to keep the call going forward toward the intended goals while addressing potential objections if they come up.

With a Z-Plan, or Zero (defensive) Plan, the objective is to slow the call from going backwards. While Janet's Pre-Call Plan didn't get into this, it can be beneficial to anticipate deal-breaker scenarios. An example in Janet's case: Say that when the Arachnid team arrived to present to the directors, two key Directors were absent, but the team was encouraged to present anyway. This would mean perhaps that they were presenting without having all of the Authority in the room and hoping that someone else could adequately represent them later. I've been in this situation before, where my team traveled several hours to find that the key decision-maker would be absent from the presentation. Thanks to having a Z-Plan, we gracefully rescheduled.

B-Plan—how the call could derail, what trigger would indicate the problem, and what to do about it.

The idea of **"mood-metering"** is to gauge how invested and agreeable an audience will be. Much like a director sets the stage and score of a movie to put the audience in a desired frame of mind before delivering the climax, your salesperson's intended agenda should take feelings, mood and energy into account. Will the audience be emotionally moved from one topic to the next in order to receive the salesperson's next proposition favorably?

Mood-metering walks through the entire agenda, considering each point from the perspective of the prospect, and identifying what their mood will be toward you and your capabilities. Are they personally interested in what's being presented? Does the agenda stimulate their excitement from start to finish or will they start to get bored and distracted along the way? For example, like many other salespeople, Janet's agenda jumped right into presentation mode. Rolland recognized this and coached her on how a presentation should start with the client in mind, starting with reminding them of their BANTC.

To get a room emotionally invested from the beginning, it's important to recap what you know about their BANTC. Specifically reminding them of their stated needs and foreshadowing your presentation based on how you'll address those needs allows the audience to find relevance in what you're about to share. Otherwise, they'd simply be listening to what *you want to say* instead of connecting the dots to what *they want to hear*.

From there, the final factor to address is whether the plan in place fully leverages **relevant sales tools**. Sales tools come in all forms from brochures and spec reports to inviting a client onsite for a tour. Fellow team members, a sales manager or a technical resource can also be sales "tools." When another person is brought along, it's important to follow the best practices of a 4-Legged Sales Call.

4-Legged Sales Calls

4-LEGGED SALES CALLS CAN BE USEFUL MEANS OF ORCHESTRATING A Ride-Along with a new salesperson. They can add value to a presentation when the opportunity is large enough to warrant all hands on deck. Janet was prepared to make her presentation into a 4-Legged Sales Call by bringing Enrique along to boost the experience Arachnid had in the room and to share a relevant case study. Rolland suggested taking the idea even further by including a sales engineer to handle technical details and questions.

The biggest challenge of 4-Legged Sales Calls is understanding and maintaining individual roles. It's unsettling to watch a salesperson nosedive during a sales call. Since we all think we are the best at whatever we do, there often comes a point during a call when we'll think the salesperson needs to be rescued. On the other hand, as we saw with Janet's first Ride-Along in this story, the salesperson may feel they have something to prove and cut in whenever they perceive an opportunity to demonstrate their expertise. Rolland pointed out, "As part of this plan, it will be important to clearly define what each of your roles are." Monroe added, "Think of it like running a basketball offense. You need to know who has the ball at any given time and when it's appropriate to pass it around."

Janet was much more team-focused when presenting to Hallmark. Since she had pre-planned each person's role and involvement, she was able to conduct the presentation seamlessly and introduce each of her fellow presenters when the moment was right. By understanding their role, each member of the presentation team recognized when it was their turn to present or answer a specific question. There were smooth transitions and hand-offs from one team member to another. No one felt the need to hog the ball and nobody hijacked someone else's role thinking they could do a better job by adding a new piece. It takes just as much trust and respect to pull off a successful 4-Legged Sales Call as it does planning.

> It takes just as much trust and respect to pull off a successful 4-Legged Sales Call as it does planning.

While Rolland didn't participate in this presentation, **Ride-Alongs** are another version of 4-Legged Sales Calls. The main purpose for a Ride-Along is for direct observation to inform your debriefing and coaching efforts. Seeing how a salesperson performs in the field allows a manager to pinpoint more accurately what their strengths and weaknesses are. It also allows managers to get out, explore the territory, and get a sense of what's going on from the lips of the customers.

When scheduling these, you can give the salesperson a heads-up or go along spontaneously. Managers often ask which approach is best, and that really depends on their goals for the Ride-Along. If they are looking to give the salesperson a test, then an unannounced Ride-Along will create more of an Accountability atmosphere. If they want to better inform their coaching and sample a variety of calls at different stages of the funnel, then planning ahead with the salesperson will be better for arranging a full day with different prospects.

In both situations, it's equally important to communicate your roles with each other as well as with the client. You don't have to come up with an elaborate story to cover up the fact that you're observing your rep and getting a better understanding of the territory. Let the salesperson lead the conversation by introducing you and explaining how you're along to see how things are going in the field. Then you can establish rapport with the customer and can explain why you'll be observing rather than participating actively. At the end of a call, the car ride back is a great opportunity to perform a Post-Call Debrief as we discussed in Chapter 5, since the details of the meeting will be very fresh in the salesperson's mind. Always begin these debriefs by asking what went well and then follow the format outlined in the Post-Call Debrief takeaway.

You may have noticed the domino effect in the last chapter. Janet's success in the end was not a fluke. It was the result of following an intentional system with purposeful meetings. She recognized through her **Activity Review** with Rolland that she could be better leveraging **4-Legged Calls** to advance her deals. With that knowledge, she incorporated a role for Enrique into her **Pre-Call Plan**. The **Pre-Call Planning Meeting** added Marcus to the mix and allowed her to extend her strategies and agenda to gain stronger confidence from the IT directors.

Through proper preparation, the presentation was a huge victory. As a sales manager, when you are having the right discussions (the right meetings), each interaction with your team (the agendas of those meetings) will inform the next one down the line. If you implement one single part of this whole communication strategy, it will have a positive impact. However, it's by using the complete communication strategy that you will see the greatest results.

Overview of the Concepts in This Chapter

» **Meeting Cadence**

- Structure
  - ◦ Consistency in timing both from a scheduling and

length-of-meeting perspective
- ◦ Each agenda should have a unique purpose so that meetings always offer value to the salesperson
- Agendas align with each wall in the Balloon Model
  - ◦ **Support** – Pre-Call Plan, Post-Call Debrief, Sales Focus Blueprint, Sales Team Meeting, and One-On-One Mentoring
  - ◦ **Accountability** – Activity Review, Funnel Review, and One-On-One Debrief

» **Activity Review**

- **Frequency** – can be monthly or quarterly depending on tenure
- Spotting Trends
  - ◦ **Overall Effort Level** – Is the salesperson working in alignment with prior commitments and expectations?
  - ◦ **Effort Level by Type of Activity** – Is the salesperson focusing their energy across all activities, or are they giving preference to some activities over others?
  - ◦ **Effort Level by Revenue Stream** – Has the salesperson found significant success in a single stream and therefore put off efforts in other areas of their plan?
  - ◦ **Success Ratios Between Activity Types and Revenue Streams** – Is the salesperson experiencing higher or lower conversion ratios than expected that need to be adjusted accordingly?
  - ◦ **Timing** – Is the salesperson balancing their time and efforts between the top and bottom of the sales funnel as appropriate?
- Discover what adjustments may be needed to improve results
- Tenure of the salesperson will impact how directly the manager is involved is determining solutions
- Validate Commitment to Changes

» **Pre-Call Plan**

- Hold on a Case-by-Case Basis

- ◦ For more impactful sales calls
- ◦ For newer/lower Balloon level salespeople
- Salespeople Should Prepare by Putting Their Overview on Paper
  - ◦ Status of relationship and BANTC
  - ◦ Agenda for the call
  - ◦ Goal of the call
  - ◦ ABZ Plan strategies
- Top Factors to Review in the Meeting
  - ◦ What stage of the funnel is the deal in?
  - ◦ Do the intended goals of the call align with the stage?
  - ◦ Has the salesperson fully considered ABZ Plan strategies?
  - ◦ Does the agenda follow an appropriate mood-meter?
  - ◦ Is the salesperson leveraging available sales tools?

» **4-Legged Sales Call**

- Good for Ride-Alongs and to Add Value to Major Opportunities
- Clearly Define Roles of Each Member
  - ◦ Know when to pass the ball
  - ◦ Recognize who should answer what questions, and then avoid hijacking someone else's role
- Ride-Along to inform your debriefing and coaching efforts
  - ◦ Sample for variety
  - ◦ Conduct Post-Call Debriefs Immediately

Epilogue

The Accountability Wall,
One-on-One Debrief,
and Funnel Review

WHILE READING THIS BOOK, YOU PROBABLY NOTICED THAT A SIGNIFI-cant portion of the story was about development—getting people going in the right direction. Monroe's goal was to keep Rolland growing and learning. Rolland then took the same approach with developing his sales team. If you look at the Team Balloon Model, though, the Accountability wall deserves and requires just as much attention as Development. To get predictable results as a sales manager, you must be able to trust that your salespeople will actually achieve what they say they will. If you can't trust their outputs, then you won't be able to accurately forecast sales results.

> Getting predictable results requires that you can trust your salespeople will actually achieve what they say they will.

There are three elements to establishing this trust. First, you have to believe the salespeople *know how* to generate the outcomes they've said they'll achieve. The best-laid plans still require a person having skills and capabilities to execute them. Second, you have to believe that the salesperson is personally motivated and truly *intends* to do the things they say they'll do. If they aren't personally committed to the outcomes, there will be nothing at stake for them if they don't accomplish them.

Finally, you must have *transparency*. You need to know that as any obstacles arise, everyone will be alerted in time to make appropriate course corrections. Consider a NASCAR driver. They have the skills and motivation necessary to win a race, but they still keep open lines of communication with their pit crew and chief. Race-car drivers win predictably with practiced precision, strong competitive energy, and wide-open eyes. It's the same for a successful sales manager.

The aim of this book has been to help you use the Support Wall of the Team Balloon Model to develop salespeople who will have the proper plans, the ability to act on them, and the motivation to fulfill them completely. The Accountability wall is about producing transparency, ensuring intent, and managing follow-through. We touched on the overall concept of building an Accountability Partnership in Chapter 4 and then we discussed helping the salesperson recognize and be held accountable to their Sales Focus Blueprint through the Activity Review meeting in Chapter 6.

There are two more core meetings to discuss that have to do with helping your salespeople hold *themselves* accountable. Remember, it's important to apply equal pressure to both walls. But, by leading with Support, you position your Accountability efforts in a positive way. If you apply equal pressure, but lead with Accountability, it casts a dark shadow over all your Support efforts.

> Offer tools that help salespeople hold themselves accountable rather than you being the instrument that holds them accountable.

Accountability and selling are similar. In sales, if you've properly established rapport, partnered with your customer, and collaborated with them on solutions, then closing tends to be easier. This is because the customer believes in the plan, has been honest with you, and fully intends to go forward with the solution. Closings get tricky only when you're trying to convince a customer of solutions they haven't already bought into. Any quality sales process is about the customer's best interest. So is Accountability. The Activity Review we saw in the last chapter was an accountability meeting, with observations made through the salesperson's eyes. What did they see? How did they feel about what was going on? What did they believe needed to change, if anything? Offer the tools that help them hold themselves accountable rather than be the instrument that holds them accountable. If it's done right, the salesperson will want to hold themselves accountable and you will simply need to support them.

Accountability has gotten a bad rap from managers who didn't follow this partnership principle; it becomes a laborious and emotionally taxing effort for them to be the one imposing accountability. Accountability doesn't have to be draining. If you ever find yourself imposing accountability like this, consider the Balloon Level of the salesperson you're struggling with. Often, they'll be in the Assess Balloon. Remember, though, you should actually put your *least* amount of effort into that balloon.

Have you ever played limbo? It doesn't take much for the bar-holder to blow their whistle when someone doesn't pass under successfully. That's the degree of involvement that managers should aim for with the Assess Balloon. Simply define where the bar is and enforce accountability if it's missed. Most accountability measures should happen with members of the Partner Balloon. You'll primarily be helping them stay on track with their plans. You can help them think about their actions, decisions, and mistakes through a different lens so they'll recognize if and when they start deviating from the path they've laid out for themselves.

To that end, there are two additional meetings in the ISM system to fulfill your Accountability obligations to your team: The One-on-One Debrief and The Funnel Review. They're meant to help the salesperson recognize things they may otherwise be missing to correct course and optimize results. Just as seeing your dentist or eye doctor annually reminds you to stay on top of flossing and ensures that your vision hasn't deteriorated, Accountability meetings are regular checkups on the activities your salespeople should be performing to excel at their jobs.

One-on-One Debrief Meetings

THE ONE-ON-ONE DEBRIEF MEETING COMPLEMENTS THE ACTIVITY REview. Since the Activity Review takes a bird's-eye view of the full forest of deal flow, the One-on-One Debrief looks deeper into the roots of the trees in front of you. To stay current on more deals, this should be at least a bi-weekly meeting of 30-45 minutes. A best practice is to hold these alternately with bi-weekly One-on-One Mentoring meetings. It's important not to miss these meetings or allow any rescheduling to get too far from the original date or you may start missing the chance to learn about and advise on important deals. If you miss them, they're gone.

The One-on-One debrief meeting looks like this:

- » **Review** the previous meeting's goals
- » **Allow the salesperson to share** a few success stories
- » **Investigate the facts** of your selected topics and **acquire insights** to inform your coaching later on
- » **Create a plan** for upcoming weeks and determine if additional **managerial involvement** is necessary
- » **Establish next meeting goals** for focus

A form that can be used to build the agenda and organize your thoughts in preparation for the One-On-One debrief can be downloaded from the book's Companion Resource website—www.acultureofpredictablesales.com.

Each debrief should open and close with a discussion of short-term goals. These goals are not activities that salespeople should spend time tracking daily. That would be leaning toward micro-management. They are the few, most important targets that the salesperson believes to be the catalysts for their other objectives in the coming weeks: What were the three key things they identified in the previous meeting that would move the meter with their sales? Did they accomplish them? Then at the end of the meeting, what are the *new* three targets they are going to work toward for advancing their deals before the next One-on-One Debrief meeting? At this point, you're just *reviewing* with the salesperson, which, if you'll recall, is Key 2 of the Accountability Partnership. But if a salesperson starts missing their targets more frequently, then this meeting is the time to ask if they think anything would help them stay on track more effectively.

As a consultant, I had such a conversation with a company president. When we met for our coaching meetings, we would end by having him identify his key short-term goals. Frequently, however, these goals hadn't been addressed before our next meeting.

So, I asked him, "I know you have many important requirements and competing obligations that take your time every day. At the same time, when you and I are together you identify things that you believe to be the important items needing your focus. What can we do to at least increase your frequency of being able to fit in these focus items that you've committed to do?"

We came up with a plan. Each week he would write down his five highest priorities, post them on the wall behind his desk, and review that list at the end of each day. He came to base his success for the day solely on whether he was able to cross any of them off. Whether or not he accomplished many other things during that day, for those few minutes crossing a priority off the list was the gauge that mattered most. This process of writing his goals down and taking a moment to remind himself of their importance helped immensely.

While the opening and closing bookends of the meeting are standardized, the body of the meeting depends on the specifics of the deals the salesperson has been working on. To **prepare** yourself for this, you should review **what they've been working on**, any **activities reports** they've provided, or other **notes taken about their performance** since the last meeting. This lets you identify specific deals or issues that need attention. While you're selecting topics, consider the following:

» Do any of their deals seem to require deeper BANTC digging?
» Is the salesperson attempting to advance a deal to the next stage of the sales process?
» Will any of the deals provide you with competitive insight?
» Do any of the deals indicate a development need for the salesperson?

You're looking into the details of the deals, so you can recognize where your salesperson might benefit from further development to improve their odds of future success. If you simply want to review the particulars of a deal for the sake of closing that deal, you should schedule a separate Pre-Call Plan Meeting.

To better coach salespeople on reading the sale, start by learning how they currently form their perceptions of the sale.

Before you can direct the conversation to your own agenda, however, start on a positive note and find out what they want to share with you. Letting the salesperson share news or success early in the meeting lets them know that you care about their accomplishments. It also helps you assess what they think is important and lay the groundwork before you attempt to challenge their perspectives later on; they'll understand you're doing so because you're in their corner.

From there, dig into the facts of the topics you want to discuss. Ask targeted questions to understand the foundation of what may be a rose-tinted perspective. Does the salesperson have an accurate understanding of BANTC, or are they misinterpreting conversations? What has the client actually said to them? Don't just uncover how a salesperson perceives a deal. Try understanding their perception so you can better coach them on better ways to read a sale.

If the salesperson suggests a deal has moved to the next stage of the sales process, check whether they've fulfilled all the requirements of the last stage. This is your opportunity to get to the heart of the details. Does your salesperson have a clear understanding of next steps? Is there a need to collaborate with them and schedule a Pre-Call Plan because a particular deal warrants a longer discussion?

You want to ensure that your salesperson is being thorough. You aren't looking to hold them back from advancing deals and closing sales, but to share the wisdom of your experience to maximize their likelihood of success. Be alert for opportunities to coach and to acquire insights about the marketplace. Are you or they noticing new industry trends that you'd like more information on? Your salespeople are your eyes and ears in the field. So, hearing about challenges or what's working for them will inform your coaching efforts in other areas and keep you relevant with your team.

Close your meeting by working with your salesperson to identify their top three goals that they should focus on in the coming weeks. Finally, have your salesperson take their own notes during the meeting and email you a copy of them afterwards. We all tend to remember more of what we write down by hand, and this also provides the opportunity to confirm that everyone is on the same page.

Funnel Review Meetings

THE REMAINING ACCOUNTABILITY-BASED MEETING WE'RE GOING TO COVER is the Funnel Review. The purpose of the meeting is to ensure the accuracy of the pipeline. While there wasn't explicitly a Funnel Review meeting in the story, when Dom, Rolland, and Monroe were in their final meeting discussing the forecast, the fact that they were confident about the figures is a direct result of having consistently held these meetings. Rolland expressed that there was a higher level of predictability associated with the deals that were included. If you want predictable results, then sales reports have to accurately reflect what's happening with each salesperson's funnel. This is achieved by reviewing each deal's BANTC Discovery status: whether it's in the **correct stage**, how appropriate the identified **next steps** are, and if any deals need to be **disqualified** from the pipeline completely.

The Funnel Review places all deals under a microscope and challenges the evidence surrounding them. It's a valuable—and anxiety-inducing—process for salespeople. Having to provide cold hard facts can be intimidating, but you need to remove emotion from the picture, and make sure your salespeople are ready and able to defend their assumptions with facts. By challenging for factual, objective evidence while avoiding blame and not allowing emotions to cloud judgment, you'll have a more open, honest, and transparent conversation with your salesperson.

This meeting is essential for generating predictable sales results because it is the one time where you really get to critically evaluate each salesperson's funnel. The timing of the meeting should depend on the length of your sales cycle. If a single sale can take a month or more to close, then conduct this meeting monthly with each salesperson. If you sell something in just a week's time, then hold shorter funnel reviews more frequently so that you stay current with existing deals. There is also an adaption of the Funnel Review in the ISM System for sales cycles as short as a day or less.

Several factors can hinder a salesperson's success and the predictability of their results. Natural optimism can misguide their interpretation of BANTC Discovery and the stage of a deal. A refusal to admit defeat can lead them to waste time chasing dead deals. Sometimes the next steps in the sales process that lead toward a close haven't been clearly defined. Brad was a huge culprit of this early in the story. He spent too much time in meetings that barely advanced his deals.

Spotlighting these issues will allow the salesperson to better recognize correct actions. They'll spend their time more efficiently instead of spinning their wheels and/or believing they're going to get results that are actually quite unlikely.

Begin the meeting by discussing the deals closest to the bottom of the funnel. These deals are the most exciting for the salesperson: they have the most potential of closing, and they are the most likely to impact the near-term sales forecast. The Funnel Review is all about getting real and facing brutal, objective truths. You should validate all the details of the deal with the salesperson, and make sure they're considering the customer's perspective. After you've covered the deals at the bottom, move up their funnel. While your focus is deal validation, you should still identify developmental opportunities to be addressed later in One-on-One Mentoring or One-on-One Debrief meetings.

> The Funnel Review is all about getting real and facing brutal, objective truths.

This meeting should help your salespeople think more critically about what *evidence* exists to support their assumptions and how they can better allocate their time. Both of you want the funnel to generate predictable results. For you, the better the odds of success, the more accurate your forecast will be. For them, their personal goals are dependent on maximizing their sales and optimizing their time.

As you prepare for your Funnel Review Meetings, keep in mind what level you are at on the Coaching Spectrum with each salesperson and act accordingly. For higher-level, more independent salespeople, that means using guiding questions to direct their thinking so that they connect the dots on their own as opposed to you pointing out the flaws with their deals directly. You also want to project the fact that you're partners, so that conclusions are being drawn collectively with inclusive language like "What are *we* going to do?" There are many types of questions you can use here, some of which were covered in Chapter 2.

Assumptive questions come from a place of believing that your salesperson is using best practices and following the sales process, but they still specify enough detail to reveal whether something isn't quite right. For example, if you wanted to confirm that a salesperson is not prematurely advancing a deal to the proposal stage, you could ask, "And what were you able to get them to commit to in exchange for a proposal?"

Evidentiary questions are useful when your gut isn't quite settled with what you've heard so far. Say your salesperson insisted that their contact is pulling the deal along and parting seas for your company. To get past the salesperson's feelings, ask "Other than what she has told you herself, what have you heard from other contacts at the company that confirms she is really an active advocate?"

Another type of question to keep up your sleeve is a **Commitment-based question**. Sometimes, during a Funnel Review, you need to get a salesperson to agree that a deal is dead and ought to be pulled from the pipeline. You could ask, "By what date will you be convinced that this deal has stalled if it hasn't closed yet?" That puts a definite end date for the deal to close—or a concession that the deal isn't going anywhere.

MANY MANAGERS MISUNDERSTAND ACCOUNTABILITY. THEY IMPOSE IT AFter sales numbers come in below expectations and simply tell their team that they didn't do enough. This isn't sustainable, nor does it lead to better results next time. There needs to be a plan established first, so sales people know where the bar is (The Sales Focus Blueprint). Through the Development wall, make sure the salesperson has the proper skill and motivation to execute the plan. From there, helping them hold themselves accountable through scheduled meetings can ensure that there is transparency with the plan and recognition of any deviations from it.

> Many managers misunderstand accountability—they simply tell their team that they didn't do enough.

I've seen many sales plans, in the absence of this type of transparency, gather dust. But by executing these last accountability meetings, as well as the previously discussed Activity Review Meeting, your team won't merely have plans in place and the skills necessary to act on them, they'll also have routines designed for nudging them back on track before failing to deliver results. Now you can trust in the outputs of your sales team, and you have the tools to make adjustments along the way to continue generating strong, predictable sales.

* * *

AUTHOR'S NOTE: *LOOK BACK OVER THE REVIEW POINTS FROM THE OTHER Takeaway chapters in this book. Look at the team you're currently managing and the challenges you're facing. Select one, or at most two strategies or meetings that you can implement now, this week. While the ISM system is designed to be used in its entirety, you'll see improvements and success from implementing even a few strategies. If you're not sure where to begin, I suggest the Team Balloon Model. By identifying where your team members fit into the model, you'll know where you should start allocating most of your time.*

As a sales manager, how you spend your time—the activities, metrics and models you focus on, as well as the team members in which you invest the most of yourself—will ultimately be what determines your success. Use the tools in this book to help you make choices from an informed strategic perspective, rather than a reactionary one, and you'll be amazed at how much easier it is to work with your team and reach your goals. A culture of predictable sales will emerge.

Overview of the Concepts in This Chapter

» **Balancing pressure between the Support and Accountability Walls**

- Lead with Development
- Trust in outputs by ensuring three elements:
  - **Skills and Capabilities**
  - **Personal Motivation and True Intent**
  - **Transparency**
- Accountability produces transparency, ensures intent, and manages follow-through

» **One-on-One Debrief Meetings**

- Bi-weekly, 30-45-minute meeting scheduled opposite the One-on-One Mentoring Mentoring
- Prepare for the meeting by selecting the deals and issues you'd like to cover
- Agenda:
  ○ Review previous meeting's goals
  ○ Allow the salesperson to share a few success stories
  ○ Investigate the facts of your selected topics and acquire insights to inform your coaching later on
  ○ Create a plan for upcoming weeks and determine if additional managerial involvement is necessary
  ○ Establish next meeting goals for focus

» **The Funnel Review Meetings**

- Timing is adjustable depending on the length of your sales cycle
- Most heavily Accountability-based meeting
  ○ Places every deal in the salesperson's funnel under a microscope in order to reveal the objective truths
  ○ Avoid emotions in order to stay focused on facts and the strength of supporting evidence
- Used to inform the sales forecast, so accuracy is vital
- Start from the bottom of the funnel and work your way up
- Use guiding questions and inclusive language as your tools for maintaining a sense of partnership amidst the evaluation
  ○ **Assumptive Questions**
  ○ **Evidentiary Questions**
  ○ **Commitment-based Questions**

Michael Andersen, MBA, CPBC

Creator of the breakthrough system Intentional Sales Management™, coach, trainer, and speaker Michael Andersen helps company leaders stuck with uninspiring revenue generate strong, predictable sales results.

As a nationwide leading sales coach and fractional CSO, he is known for his ability to ask the right questions and then integrate unique market positioning with proven best practices. His books and talks focus on providing actionable insights that help produce immediate results.

Michael has been starting and growing businesses since the 3rd Grade. While earning his MBA, he founded what would become the largest mid-market CRM implementation company in North America.

Seeing the challenges facing sales and marketing teams, he realized the true gold in transforming sales was not in technology solutions. Instead, it lay in developing better sales strategies and improving personnel training and management.

With this new direction in mind, Michael sold the company in 2007 to focus on consulting, coaching, and training. He has since become a go-to resource for businesses and private equity firms seeking top-shelf expertise in sales turnaround.

He has partnered with executive and sales leadership of hundreds of companies in numerous industries, from Fortune 100 enterprises to successful family-run businesses. They turn to his expertise to build and train their sales departments, develop their sales processes, and transform their go-to-market strategies.

Find out more at CultureOfSalesSolutions.com.